A Life of Salvation

Inspired By God
Written by Cecil E. Barry,
Servant of God the Father and our Lord Jesus Christ

The purpose of the book is to provide the reader an understanding of what God planned from the beginning of time, what happened to His plan, and what He is planning
in the end.

Table of Contents

Acknowledgments

I want to thank God the Father and our Lord Jesus Christ for spending so much time teaching me and giving me the contents of this book to share with others while it administered to my soul in teaching me about spiritual transformation and change. I would like to thank all who have been patient with me as I shared the content of this book as each piece was being brought forth. I would like to thank the members of the Bible Study Fellowship group at SPE for supporting me and allowing me to use them as a testing ground for the material in this book. Special thanks to Jana Mason for helping to inspire me to seek God's will in regard to presenting God's teachings. The beautiful cover of this book is all due to the great talent and skills of Allan Jones, who took an image from my daughter's work, and created a master piece. I could not have completed this book without the work and dedication I received from Adam Wilson, who worked with me to bring this book together and get me through the layout and publishing process. And to my dear wife Donna, who spent so many hours reviewing this material, all glory to God.

Preface

The contents of this book has been a culmination of many years of studying scriptures, listening to the teaching of Jesus Christ, and receiving understanding through the Holy Spirit. When I accepted my calling, I thought that I needed to join a church and receive teaching from a pastor. But our Lord Jesus Christ reminded me of the following scripture:

> - *Jeremiah 31:33–34 (NLT)—"'But this is the new covenant I will make with the people of Israel on that day,' says the Lord. 'I will put my instructions deep within them, and I will write them on their hearts. I will be their God, and they will be my people. And they will not need to teach their neighbors, nor will they need to teach their relatives, saying, "You should know the Lord." For everyone, from the least to the greatest, will know me already,' says the Lord."*

And the Holy Spirit pointed me to this scripture:

> - *John 14:26 (NLT)—"But when the Father sends the Advocate as my representative—that is, the Holy Spirit—he will teach you everything and will remind you of everything I have told you."*

He revealed to me that my road to gaining understanding was in developing a direct and close relationship with him. So I spent the next eight years studying and listening to his teachings. There is nothing special about me personally; it was just my calling to receive instructions and guidance from Jesus Christ and the Holy Spirit directly. Others may be called to receive their calling directly or through a religious organization. Please do what the Lord is calling you to do and everything will be all right. I have developed relationships with Pastor Lee Edwards of Kingdom Life Fellowship and (Pastor) Dr. Timothy J. Wilbert of Bible Way Community Baptist Church, who both have helped me to understand operational processes in leading and running a church.

As time went by, I was focused on allowing the Holy Spirit to clean up my life. I spent very little time speaking to others about what Christ was teaching me. Until one day God asked me a question: "Do you think all the things I have taught and poured into you are only for you? He instructed me to start sharing the teachings; He shared with me a vision into what will be the completion of my assignment. This book is the beginning of the work I have been called to share. I pray that it blesses you as you read and study its contents. You will need your Bible to work through the content of this book.

The goal of this book is to share five key areas where we have lost our focus in seeking God's perspective and will:
  • Understanding "God's Plan of Salvation"
  • Sharing about our Lord Jesus Christ "The Christ"
  • Sharing how we "Learn to Overcome"
  • Understanding what it means to obtain "Spiritual Transformation"
  • Sharing how we live a "Life of Salvation"

As I grew closer and closer in my relationship with God the Father and our Lord Jesus Christ, I became aware of how much I really did not understand. As we are taught in the Bible, I started to draw closer to God by seeking Him in every way. As a young man, I knew that I had an assignment that God wanted me to complete. Instead of seeking and allowing God to reveal my assignment, I requested time to go and take part in all that the world had to offer. In retrospect, I should have just answered the calling at that time, and things would have been a lot easier than what I had to go through once I turned back to God. Once I accepted and started to believe in my destiny, things began to change. Now, we all know that things just didn't change overnight. Because of the sin that I had allowed into my nature, a cleansing process was needed to prepare me for service. It took about eight years for God to reveal things to me that He wanted to be gone out of my life and for Him to confirm that I was ready to be sent out to teach. I know, what a long time of preparing someone; but, it's God's timetable and not mine or yours. I do understand why it took so long; God wanted to make sure that I had actually put to death all the sin He had identified in me. Not that I am sinless, but the sin that was identified was causing an issue with my relationship with God. I had to pass the test for each one. It just took some time to work through all the transgressions, disciplining, gaining understanding, testing, failing, gaining understanding, and then passing the test, for me to get to this point in life and my relationship with God the Father and our Lord Jesus Christ.

While I was being cleansed, God was pouring His teaching into me. This is the first of three books that have been revealed for me to write. I hope the teaching that has been given to me, enlightens your spirit and creates a renewed desire in you to develop a closer and personal relationship with God the Father and our Lord Jesus Christ. I pray that each person who reads this book embarks on a lifetime of spiritual transformation and seeks the full experience and measure of God's salvation, as we are led to become more like Christ in these last days.

God's Plan from the Beginning

Chapter 1

Gods Plan from the Beginning

From the very beginning, God developed a plan to create a group of people who would look to Him for instruction and guidance. God the Father wants a group of people who will praise and worship Him, not because of what He can do for them, but for what His people will accomplish through His plan. From the beginning, God put His Spirit in place to help lead His people through His plan. God, through our Lord Jesus Christ, created the perfect environment for man and woman to exist. Everything was provided for them, and all they had to do was take care of what God provided and follow a very simple rule. If man would simply have done what God required, things would have been a whole lot different today. But, even today, we refuse to fear, reverence, praise, and worship God in the correct way. Let's take a look at what God planned and what God plans to do to accomplish with what He put in place and what He will do to complete His plan.

God Appointed Christ over Earth, Man, and Woman

As we learn in the Bible, it was God the Father's plan from the beginning to put Jesus Christ in place as our God and Savior. Before God the Father placed everything under the feet of Jesus Christ, He stated that He would humble all of Christ's enemies under his feet and make them a footstool to Christ. (Psalms 110:1)

Christ came down from heaven to experience the things that man experiences as a human so he would know what it meant to be a man and he could have compassion and love for us because of our weaknesses. Jesus Christ clearly understood his mission, which was to accomplish what God the Father had planned. In the book of John, Jesus tells us that, even before Abraham was born, Jesus Christ existed with the Father. (John 8:57–59)

God the Father has been working His plan of Salvation for man from the very beginning. It was His plan to create prophets to introduce God's instructions and guidance to His people. It was God's plan to send His son to be the savior of the world. No man could have completed God's plan. No amount of sacrifice from man would have completed God's plan. It took someone from heaven that was not subject to human nature and who was without sin. Because of Jesus Christ's obedience to the Father, he has inherited God's power and authority. It was a part of God's plan to create the universe through His son. Jesus Christ is the radiant glory of God the Father, and he is looking to cleanse those who trust in him from sin.

God's Plan from the Beginning

Christ came and created the Church, Disciples, and Apostles, and provided access to the Holy Spirit to those who place their faith and trust in him. Not only has Christ been given control over God's people, but God the Father has made his name greater than any other name in heaven. (Hebrews 1:1–4)

Just like we don't know the origin of God the Father, we also don't know the origin of Christ. We have been taught that Christ was born from the Virgin Mary, but if we study the Bible carefully, we will come to know that Christ existed before the world was created because it was through Christ that the Father created all things. It is a part of God's plan to position Jesus Christ as our God, and provide him a throne on which he could rule over God's people. God the Father knows that Jesus Christ will demonstrate justice in his governing of God's people and how much Christ loves justice and hates evil. We come to understand that Jesus Christ has been anointed as our God and that he is higher in heaven than anyone else except the Father himself. We have a true God, through which all the goodness of the Father flows to us. (Hebrews 1:8–9)

Now that we can agree through scripture that God had a plan from the beginning, which included the coming of Christ, the death of Christ, and the anointing of Christ as our God over God the Father's people, we can focus on the plan of God without working to divide the Body of Christ. For we know it is through Christ that God the Father brings the fullness of his glory upon man. It is only through us fully accepting the position that

God's Plan from the Beginning

Christ has come to receive from God the Father that we can understand His plan of salvation.

God Creates the Heaven, Earth, Man, and Woman

We can now take a look at how God, through His great power, wisdom, and our Lord Jesus Christ, created the heaven, earth, man, and woman. *God Created the World and Prepared it for Man:* We read in the book of Genesis that God prepared the earth for man to inhabit. He created a plan that would be self-sufficient without any help from man. The planet produced all sorts of vegetation, plants, trees, and fruit. (Genesis 1:9)

God Prepared Everything We Needed to Prosper: When you look at the position and environment that God placed Adam in (the Garden of Eden), Adam had everything that he needed. God would actually anticipate the needs of Adam before Adam requested them. He created woman because he was watching over Adam and his needs. When we think about God's prosperity, when we are in His will, there is nothing we actually need to labor to achieve. Even when God moved Israel out of Egypt, he took them to a land already prepared for his people; they did not have to work to live in the prosperity that God prepared for them. But, today, we are looking for the wrong type of prosperity; we want it to come from our labor, our own knowledge, or education. We pray that God just blesses us in whatever we do. This is the beginning of our troubles.

God Created Man and Woman: From the start, God demonstrated how much he wanted us to work within His will, so He created us in His image so we could be called children of God (Genesis 1:27)

God Gave Us All Authority Over What He Created With Instructions for Us to Multiply: After making us in His image, He gave us full control over all that He had created for the purpose of multiplying His blessings so He would receive all the glory and we would be blessed. (Genesis 1:28)

God's Plan from the Beginning

God Provided Us Food to Sustain Us: When God had finished with all His work and all the things He created, including putting man in position as caretaker and manager, God was pleased with all His creations. He determined that it was all good. (Genesis 1:29–31)

God Prepared a Place for Man to Live: God decided that He would prepare a place for man and woman to live. He created the Garden of Eden, just for man and woman. This was a very beautiful place, created by God with all His love and compassion. (Genesis 2:8–10)

God Populated the Garden of Eden to Make it Sustainable: God then created all kinds of animals and birds. He turned these animals over to man to manage and name them. (Genesis 2:19)

God Gave Us a Very Simple Rule to Follow: After all the work that God had done, He decided to rest. He then warned man and woman not to partake of the tree of life. (Genesis 1:16–17)

Now this is true love. How many of us today would have done what God completed for man? If we had the power of God, what would we really do with it? To pour into man all His love and compassion, to create a very beautiful place, not for himself, but for those who did not love Him.

God creates some to be Righteous, Some to be Unrighteous

I have to tell you this section created a new understanding in me, as God continued to teach me his ways and reveal his plan of salvation. It's one thing to believe we were all born of sin; it's another thing to understand that some were created to bring about sin and others to demonstrate His glory. More important, is the question was I one of those created for God to demonstrate sin to others? We all need to demonstrate faith and overcome to receive salvation.

God's Plan from the Beginning

Those Righteous from Birth: I came to understand that God chooses certain people to receive His salvation from birth; these people come to understand their assignment from the very beginning. They are not those who have been in church all their lives and then turn to be part of this world; these people are set apart from the start. They have never strayed from God and His plan for their lives. From the start, they accepted the lifestyle that brings them very little riches and glory. Their focus from the start was/is to please God. Their life is free from sin; they have experienced the fullness of God the Father and Jesus Christ. At an early age, they never turned away from God and his calling.

We all know the story of Noah. God was very disappointed about creating man because, with all that God had provided man, man still refused to accept God and His ways. God decided that He would destroy the world because of the sin of man. But there was a man who had found favor with God. Noah did not live in sin as other men. He lived a righteous life before God and was blameless before man. Can you imagine being the only person that God is looking toward to continue his plan of salvation. When God gave Noah his assignment, no one else believed the assignment that God had given Noah. Those who are born to be righteous have a calling that will cause them to live differently than others who are living in sin. (Genesis 6:7–9)

Samuel was another one from birth who dedicated his life to God. God developed a relationship with Samuel and called upon him for an assignment to judge and guide God's people. As God worked in Samuel, many people came to learn that God was with Samuel. The people went to Samuel, requesting that he anoint someone king over them because that was the custom of the land. Samuel refused and sought out God's guidance and instructions, in which God directed Samuel to anoint Israel a king. Those born in a righteous state do not allow others to defile them, based on the ways of this world or the sinful desires of others. (1 Samuel 3:19)

God's Plan from the Beginning

Isaiah was a very impressive man of God. He, like Noah and Samuel, knew God from birth and like them; He was created for a special assignment. Each one worked from the beginning to complete their godly assignment. Isaiah's assignment was to confront the kings of Israel and Judah. This was a tough assignment because he had to instruct and guide God's people through a king. God requested for Isaiah to walk around for three years naked and barefoot to be an example of the troubled times that were coming upon Egypt and Ethiopia. Isaiah also went to King Hezekiah to warn him that God was going to cause him to die through the illness he was suffering from. Through Isaiah's interactions with King Hezekiah, the king repented and God added 15 years to his life. Isaiah prophesied about the coming of John the Baptist, and he prophesied about the coming of Christ. (Isaiah 49:1–4)

John the Baptist was another person chosen from birth to complete a very important assignment of God. John was tasked with preparing the way for Christ and to warn the people to repent and turn to God for the forgiveness of sin. John developed disciples to follow the way of God. When John encountered Jesus Christ, he was assigned the task of baptizing Christ. As with most of those called from birth to serve God, John cared very little about his possessions or money. He walked around wearing camel's hair and a leather belt, and he ate locusts and wild honey for food. Another aspect of those called from birth is in the way they die. John the Baptist was beheaded by King Herod, who loved listening to John. Jesus Christ makes a statement that there is no one born of woman greater than John the Baptist; yet, if we can make it into the Kingdom of God in these last days, we will be greater than he. (Luke 1:11–15)

God has a plan to create some righteous and some who are unrighteous; this is all part of His ultimate plan. Those who are created unrighteous have to overcome and be transformed into the Body of Christ.

God's Plan from the Beginning

- Romans 9:20–22 (NIV)—"But who are you, O man, to talk back to God? 'Shall what is formed say to him who formed it, "Why did you make me like this?" ' Does not the potter have the right to make out of the same lump of clay some pottery for noble purposes and some for common use? What if God, choosing to show his wrath and make his power known, bore with great patience the objects of his wrath—prepared for destruction."

We know that God desires everyone to receive salvation. Those who are not chosen from birth to receive an assignment from God can still be chosen to bring God glory by allowing God to snatch us out of the fire, which is meant for destruction. Most of us fall into this category; we must repent and surrender our lives over to Christ and we too can experience the salvation of God and be made for useful work and assignment. Let's look at a few in the Bible who experienced salvation is this manner.

The Unrighteous Who are Called into Righteous Living: A good example of someone who was not selected from birth was David. Because of the disobedience of Saul, God had to select another person to continue leading God's people. Even though Saul had turned away from God, thus causing God to turn away, David continued to honor the assignment that God had given to Saul. A demonstration of God being with David was the defeat of Goliath. David learned how to seek God's instruction and guidance to lead God's people. God blessed David in all his battles and gave David rest from all his enemies. Unlike those who from birth are called to serve God, these individuals have to overcome things in their life. David fell into temptation when he looked upon Bathsheba. To compound the issue, David planned the death of Bathsheba's husband, Uriah. David then had to confess his sins and repent. Even though God forgave David, he and his family had to pay the consequences for David's sin. Many of us are like this today; even after God has called us, we still walk in or surrender to temptation, which makes us fall short of the will of God. The difference I see between these two groups of people is the desire to surrender totally to God the Father and our Lord Jesus Christ. It seems those who have given their life to

God's Plan from the Beginning

God from the beginning don't fall into temptation like those who are called out of the fire. Jesus Christ encouraged us to stop sinning, but we continue to reason that we cannot stop. We continue to sin, thinking God's grace will always cover our sins no matter what we do. But we must seek the truth in Christ and overcome our ungodly ways and thinking so we can live in confidence and make it through the fire. (1 Samuel 16:1)

Another person who was called out of the fire was the Apostle Paul. After spending years killing God's people, Paul was called by Christ to become a key servant. Many of us have to experience this same type of dramatic life changing experience. We are so deep into sin that God has to incorporate a very powerful event or incident that causes us to rethink our reason for living. Our hearts have grown so hard against the Word of God and Jesus Christ that there is nothing anyone can preach to get us to change our ways. Yes, we attend church, but we won't surrender our life over to Jesus Christ. One thing that is common to those who are called to serve from birth and those called out of the fire is the suffering that both must undergo for God. Paul experienced many years of suffering to help bring others to God the Father and Christ Jesus. Another thing that both groups of people share is the power of God in their lives; both groups had the ability to perform many signs and miracles. These individuals are motivated to share the Word of God, not to benefit them but to benefit those who are lost and to bring God all the glory. We also know that Paul struggled with keeping temptation out of his life and out of his thoughts and actions. If we walk in truth and continue to confess our desires as Paul shared with his readers, then we too can overcome as Paul did. God knows we will be tempted, but we must not fall into doubt and disobedience so we won't have to suffer the consequence of sin. These consequences could affect us, our family, friends, and others. Paul had the love of God in his heart and knew how to fight and run a good race for Christ. We know that, in the end, Paul completed his assignment and died in confidence that he would be raised with Christ. (Acts 9:7–9)

God's Plan from the Beginning

Those called into righteous standing from birth and those who are called into righteous standing from out of the fire have things in common, such as the love of God and our Lord Jesus Christ. These individual have learned how to live by faith and not by sight. They understand God's plan of salvation and their part in His plan. There is nothing in this world someone could give them to get them to give up what they have experienced in God and Jesus Christ.

God Establishes His Covenants with Man

God's plan of salvation has always been established through the creation of a covenant. A covenant is an agreement between two parties. It establishes the rules by which the two parties will operate and the outcome of the agreement if both parties hold up their end. It also describes the negative effects if one of the parties breaks the agreement before the agreed upon period.

God Makes a Covenant with Man: Once God completed setting up a place for man and provided His rules by which we need to operate, He established a covenant with man. A covenant is a promise that God makes to give us confirmation that He will operate a certain way toward us and all the living creatures on the earth. It also describes the obligations that man has to operate in, to ensure what he does is pleasing to God and that he remains under God's covenant. (Genesis 9:12–14)

God Confirms His Covenant with Abraham: There are always two parts to any covenant. God made a promise to bless Abraham from generation to generation if he would obey God's commandments. We can trust that God will do His part in upholding the covenant; but can God trust that we will uphold our end of the covenant. As we know and will see, we continued to fail to uphold our end as part of God's plan of salvation to bless His people. (Genesis 17:7–11)

The Commandments of the Covenant: As with any agreement, there are always rules to ensure the transaction will be upheld and the parties in the agreement understand the obligations in completing the agreement. God put rules in place so the

God's Plan from the Beginning

agreement could be realized and be put into action. One great aspect of a covenant is that it can be passed down from generation to generation. Abraham passed the covenant to Isaac and Jacob. (Exodus 20:1–17)

God Makes a Covenant with Moses: Even after the convent that was established between Abraham, Isaac, and Jacob was broken, God continued to seek a person whom He would find righteous enough to establish another covenant with, so He chose Moses. As with the other covenants, God established His promises and the rules by which man had to operate. (Exodus 34:10–11)

At this point, we are all set. God has given us all that we need, put us in charge, and given us only a few commandments to follow. All we had to do was to stay with God's plan of salvation and live in His goodness. How many of us today experience God's plan in our lives but refuse to accept it "as is?" We just have to make some kind of change or adjustment. But why do we change a perfect solution? Do we have the need to be in control, even to the point of rejecting the goodness of God?

From the beginning, God already knew we would not be able to carry out His plan of salvation, so He prepared His Son to bring about a covenant that could never be broken by man's sin. This allowed God to keep His promises in place for those who are willing to accept them. We know that the covenants in the Old Testament were put in place through the sacrificing of animals, but God has provided a way for us to receive salvation through the blood of our Lord Jesus Christ. It is through the blood of Jesus Christ that we are confirmed as part of the new covenant if we believe, accept, and obey the ways of God. In the old covenant, priests were the ones delivering the word and instructions from God; but in the new covenant, our Lord and Savior Jesus Christ has become our high priest forever. In the new covenant, God's ways and word are placed in our hearts and written in our minds so that each person who accepts God's Son can be taught through God's Holy Spirit to serve Him in reverence and humbleness. Christ Jesus is the mediator of the new covenant between God and those who live on the earth. Through this new covenant and the power and authority of our Lord Jesus Christ, we can be reconciled to God. (Hebrews 9:15)

- We have choices to make: God's plan of salvation is available to those who are willing to be transformed and trust in His plan and power.
- We have a choice to make: to live for God the Father and Jesus Christ or to live for ourselves.
- We have a choice to make: to live in the light or walk in darkness.
- We have a choice to make: to walk in the love of God or in the love of man.
- We have a choice to make: to walk in godly riches or continue to seek the riches of the world.
- We have a choice to make: to walk in freedom or continue to be bound by Satan.
- We have a choice to make: to grow in faith or continue to be bound by fear.
- We have a choice to make: to be separate from this world or be destroyed by it.
- We have a choice to make: to continually seek God's face or be found in shame.
- We have a choice to make: to be free from sin or continue to be entangled in sin.
- We have a choice to make: to become a new creation or continue to perish in our current state.
- We have a choice to make: to be spiritually transformed or remain in a religious state destined for destruction.
- We have a choice to make: to be found in Christ or remain lost in this world.
- We have a choice to make: to become holy in Christ or continue in wickedness.
- We have a choice to make: to become a child of God or remain a child of Satan.
- We have a choice to make: to live through God's Spirit or die in our transgressions.
- We have a choice to make: to accept our assignment or resist our calling.
- We have a choice to make: to accept God's plan of salvation or create our own plan.

- We have a choice to make: to change our ways or enter into judgment not knowing our fate.
- We have a choice to make: to seek joy and peace or remain in our sinful nature.

Choose you this day, who you will serve? Will it be God, self, or man!

What Happened?

Even after God had taken the time to give us very specific rules to follow and communicated very clearly that, if we would just stay with His plan and gain understanding, He would protect us. But, we felt compelled to go against the will of God and devise our own way. In other cases, we thought that we could pretend to follow God's ways, but, when things became difficult, we decided not to wait on God. We moved forward and created our own plans and prayed that God would continue to bless us. Much like we do today, we spend a small amount of time on Sunday in church, a little time praying, and pay small amounts of tithes and offerings; we believe that this routine entitles us to have the ability to approach God with all kinds of requests. And when our requests are not met, we create our own way and claim that God is blessing our plans.

Man Rejects the Ways of God: Despite all the warnings from God's prophets and God choosing to send the people of Israel and Judah to Babylon for punishment, we still could not follow His ways. God extended His mercy and grace by bringing His people back to the Promised Land and rebuilding Jerusalem, and we still could not follow God's plan of salvation. The priests were busy telling lies about how God would continue to bless them if they would continue to offer sacrifices. But, God hated their sacrifices because of the great sin of the people. The priest's had left God's path, and their instructions caused the people to stumble into sin. The people of Judah were marrying those who did not believe in God. Men were unfaithful to their wives, and this displeased God. People were getting divorced and creating ungodly children. We even held back our offerings, and cheated God by our lack of giving. We then decided that there is no use in serving God, thinking nothing good would come from serving him. God shared with us His plan to send his messenger to prepare the way, and that we will be placed on trial and he will judge us to determine if we have cheated our employees, oppressed the widows and orphans, deprived the foreigners from a good life, or refused to fear God. Those who are wicked and arrogant will be burned up, but those who fear God will go free. (Malachi 2:7–9)

God Establishes a New Covenant not based on Man: No matter how many times God tried to get us to accept his plan and allow Him to lead and shower us with His great love, we decided our own ways were better. God allowed us to have free will and choice to see what decisions we will make. We have taken this blessing and covered and defiled ourselves by acting and becoming religious. Man is paying a very big price for insisting that we get our way and that God should just accept us continuing in our sinful nature.

In this and time, we should be able to read the many stories in the Old Testament and see the outcomes and consequences that others had to suffer when they utilized their freedom of choice and made bad decisions that led them away from God. Do we think things are any different for us today? Do we believe we are smarter or more advanced than those who came before us? If that is true, then we should be able to understand how all things were created in the past. We still cannot determine how pyramids were constructed, how to control the weather, or how to keep the planet from losing its resources. But, God loves us anyway. So He decided, even with all our faults, he would yet again create a new covenant with man. God wants us all to be saved and experience His plan of salvation. We need to wake up and stop thinking things we can create, imagine, or dream into existence can compare to the plan God has already prepared for those who love Him. But, even under the new covenant, we still continue to show God we don't need him for everything in our lives, so we continue to suffer even as we call on the name of the one and only Christ Jesus, the God of our new covenant in which God the Father receives glory.

God's Plan from the Beginning

God Decided to Make a Covenant through Christ: After spending many years working with man to try to get us to operate under His convent, God decided to remove man from the equation. The prophets, priests, and God's people failed to uphold man's part of the convent. For over 400 years, God tried to get us to follow His laws and instructions, but we refused to stay humble and be blessed. God then departed from man for 400 years before He decided to save man from himself. God loves us so much that He sent His Son to establish a covenant between God and man; but this time, God based our ability to receive His blessings on faith in His Son Jesus Christ and by the sacrificing of Christ's blood for our sins so we can have a lasting relationship with God. (Hebrews 12:23–25)

We Choose to Make a Name for Ourselves: Even with the new covenant in place and Christ sitting at the right hand of God, interceding for us, we still refuse to follow God's plan. We get tired of waiting on God, so we start creating our own plans. Much like when man decided to build the tower that would reach the heavens. This disobedience caused God to step in and create different languages so they could not communicate with each other. Our disobedience today is causing God to redirect and select others by which His plan can be completed. Instead of experiencing the beauty of God's plan for our lives, we continue to fight and deny the work of God that was planned for us long before we were born. (Genesis 11:4–7)

We Show Contempt and Greed for the Lord's Offering: Our religious leaders today continue the practices of the unfaithful priests which caused God's anger to manifest itself in the Old Testament—especially when it comes to dealing with the Lord's offering. We refuse to operate in God's will. We decided to change the order of when the religious leaders took their share from the offering. Again, man's disobedience caused God to step in and reject the offering of sinners. (1 Samuel 2:16–17)

We Rejected God as our King: It would seem that, once we seen God moving around on earth in fire, in a cloud, and filling His presence in tents, that we would be committed to following His directions. But, being human, we felt it would be better if another man much like ourselves would lead us. We decided to reject even the presence of God from leading us to glory. I know many of us repeat this process today. It's still hard for us to comprehend that God, who is not human, is willing to lead us to eternity. But this is God's plan and a very important part of getting His people to accept Him as God. We have spent many years suffering from the leadership of man. Why do we continue to think our deliverance from all that binds us and causes us to suffer is in the mind or control of a man? Even those who lead us today in government roles continue to disappoint us. Our bosses on our jobs, our spouses at home, and even our children can cause us to be disappointed and suffer. (1 Samuel 8:6–7)

We Don't Wait on the Lord, Even Though God has Revealed His Plan to Us: I cannot explain how important this lesson is to every believer. God has a plan for each one of us; we have to demonstrate patience and maturity in waiting on God's plan to change us and things in our lives for His glory. Even if God reveals His plan to us, we cannot take over and get tired of waiting on God. He has the perfect solution, but if we do what Saul did, we will suffer the same fate. Samuel shared a revelation from God with Saul regarding Saul becoming king. Saul was given a very simple instruction, *"Go to Gilgal and wait for me to come, and I will anoint you and offer sacrifices to God."* But Saul started to listen to those around him, and he decided that waiting on God's plan to take place was taking too long.

So he decided to offer the burnt offering himself. We must learn from lessons of long ago so we can please God today. We must demonstrate patience and allow God's plan to work in our lives so we will not fail to receive that which God has prepared for us. We all know the story of Saul; time after time, he decided to take matters into his own hands and make decisions without instructions or directions from God. In the end, God had no choice but to remove Saul as king. God is the same today as He was yesterday; He will take things away from us if we choose to not follow His plan. (1 Samuel 13:7–10)

God's Plan from the Beginning

We decide that God's Plan is not Good Enough: Even after we place our trust in God, we still try to change God's plan. Again, Saul would not accept God's perfect plan and decided that he would make a decision and change God's plan. We are warned several times in the Bible that we are not to add, modify, or change the Word of God; that includes His instructions and directions. If God instructs us to carry out a task, we must do exactly as we have been told and not change the instructions to include our own thoughts or ideals. God does not need our ideals; He just needs our faith and obedience so His plan can have massive impact on our lives and those of others. This also goes for receiving directions. If God tells us to go a certain place, don't decide some other place is better. God's knows better than us, if we can just believe! (1 Samuel 15:17–19)

God's Plan through Jesus Christ

As I have mentioned before, it was always God's plan to reveal His plan of salvation for man through His son Jesus Christ. He knew we would not be able to carry out the tasks required for us to be fully accepted. But, we demanded that God give us a king to lead us, so He did. We now know that our demand caused many to suffer and lose their lives. Thanks to the awesome and majestic glory of God, He looked past our weaknesses and revealed to us His plan for guiding us into His presence and becoming one with Him.

Christ Revealed

It is through God's Holy Spirit that He has chosen to reveal Christ to us. When we confess and believe in our heart that Jesus is the son of God and we follow the commands of God, we come to know Jesus Christ. By God revealing Christ to us, that which is in us is revealed in the light of Christ. He will reveal our deepest thoughts and desires so we can be made whole in Him. All the things that are hidden will be revealed, and Christ will clean up those who are in darkness if we give ourselves over to Christ. All the power of God the Father is revealed in Christ Jesus, and the righteous judgment of Christ will be revealed when he returns. Through Jesus Christ, God has revealed His glory and the mystery of God's plan of salvation.

> -Matthew 16:17–19 (NLT)—"Jesus replied, 'You are blessed, Simon son of John, because my Father in heaven has revealed this to you. You did not learn this from any human being. Now I say to you that you are Peter (which means "rock"), and upon this rock I will build my church, and all the powers of hell will not conquer it. And I will give you the keys of the Kingdom of Heaven.'

Christ Defeats Satan

God also knew that the hold of death on our lives would prevent us from fully giving ourselves over to Him. Another part of His plan was to have Christ overcome the sting of death that Satan held over man. There are so many people who have a fear of dying. They attend church, praise and worship God, but they are still not free from the fear of death. None of us want to die. but if death is the only way we can see the full measure of God's plan for us, then we need to accept death as part of God's plan of salvation and not view it as something that Satan can continue to cause us to fear. Actually, we need to experience death, even before our bodies actually die. Jesus and his disciples taught us that we were born in sin and that we must become a new creation while still living in the body. We are taught that all sin must be put to death so we can walk in the freedom that comes through faith and trust in Jesus Christ. Therefore, we must operate as if our bodies are already dead. If we have already died in Christ Jesus, why do we continue to fear what has already occurred? But, if we have not put our sinful nature to death, then we have some work to do. There should be a day in our lives where we come to understand that the old person we used to be has died and is buried. Oh death, where is your sting! We now live in the Body of Christ, where death has lost its sting. (1 Corinthians 15:51–57)

The Gift of Salvation

One of the main parts of God's plan is to bring salvation to those who believe in His Word, believe in Jesus Christ, and trust in Him. There are many who spend most of their time focusing on being "saved," but there is a bigger goal than God just forgiving us of our sins; it is the goal of experiencing the full salvation of God the Father and Jesus Christ. When our goal is to only get God to accept us and save us from our sins, we tend not to grow past this point. While the goal of salvation does include getting God to accept us and save us from sin, it goes further into transforming and changing us into the Spirit of Christ. As we grow in God's salvation, He continues to reveal more and more to us. We become someone he can trust with performing miracles and demonstrating the power of God through us. When we mature, by growing in God's plan of salvation, we will produce 10-, 20-, 100-fold for Christ. All that we live for is to produce something good and pleasing to God, each and every day. We no longer spend our time engrossed in the things of this world and carrying out actions that we already supposedly put to death in our sinful nature. We see the world through the eyes of Christ and the Father. Everything is done to help bring others to Christ and assist in their maturing into God's plan of salvation. We are the ones who have overcome through the blood of Christ. We don't spend our time acting religiously or trying to convince others we are religious. We live out our days seeking all that pleases God the Father and our Lord Jesus Christ.

> *- Revelation 12:10–11 (NLT)—"It has come at last—salvation and power and the Kingdom of our God, and the authority of his Christ. For the accuser of our brothers and sisters has been thrown down to earth—the one who accuses them before our God day and night. And they have defeated him by the blood of the Lamb and by their testimony. And they did not love their lives so much that they were afraid to die."*

God's Plan from the Beginning

A New Creation

Those who have spent some time listening to or reading the Word of God, have learned that those who give themselves over to Christ become a new creation. God took the time to explain to me what this entails. As I have mentioned in the above paragraph, we must all experience death to our sinful nature; and, without this process occurring, we cannot become a new creation. We have to grasp that all of the old things in our lives have passed and everything is new. This means we are not the same person and we do not indulge in sexual immorality. We are not hateful and angry people. We don't hold back from helping others because someone else has hurt us. We have control over our thoughts, feelings, and responses in all situations and circumstances. No longer do we blame others or create justifications and reasoning to satisfy our sinful nature. When we reach this point in God's plan of salvation in our lives, we are separated for the work that God has called us to complete. Those who have come this far cannot turn back and get entangled again with life's worries and cares. If we have walked with God and our Lord Jesus Christ and we have experienced the power of His awesomeness and His glory, we cannot turn back. If we do, there is no other salvation to experience. We would be crucifying Christ all over again. We know better than to turn our backs on God after He has placed His trust in us and shown us His great power. Those of us who make it to this point in God's plan of salvation are given a new name (Hebrews 6:4).

A new name is given so God no longer references you as the person who lived in a sinful state. We can take a look at a few individuals for whom God changed their names and saw them as a new creation. God renamed Abram to Abraham when he made the covenant with him. God rename Abraham's wife from Sarai to Sarah when God blessed her to be the mother of the nation of Israel. We also know that before Peter was given the assignment to build the church, his name was changed from Simon to Peter. Again, after calling Paul into his assignment to preach the gospel to the Gentiles, God changed his name from Saul to Paul. There are many others who names have been changed because they became a new creation in God the

Father and Christ, and they were assigned a life-changing task for God. Even Jesus Christ speaks of having a new name. After the time of judgment has passed, and the time for a new beginning comes, Christ will be given a new name. Those of us who reach this point in their walk with God will also be given a new name. (Revelation 2:17)

What Are God and Jesus Christ Doing?

The question we may have is what is God the Father and our Lord Jesus Christ doing? Why is there such a delay in the return of Christ Jesus? We have to remember that God the Father's goal is to create a group of people who know how to praise and worship Him; this is not a small amount of people. The more we walk contrary to God, the fewer of us will make it in. On a personal note, if we have not become a new creation in Christ, we need his coming to be delayed. We need to examine our lives in Christ truthfully. We don't want to be one of those spoken about who claimed and acted as if they were praising and worshipping God and, when judgment day comes,
Christ tells us he never knew us. That would be a very bad day. God has never stopped working His plan of salvation. Jesus Christ gives us confirmation, that he and the Father are always at work, trying to get us to accept the Word of God, the truth of God, the Son of God, and the salvation of God.

- John 5:17 (NIV)—"Jesus said to them, 'My Father is always at his work to this very day, and I, too, am working.' "

Instruction and Guidance

A part of what God the Father and Jesus Christ are doing is teaching those who surrender themselves to Jesus Christ. Back in the Old Testament, God revealed that He plans to change the way He communicates His instructions and directions. Because of the wickedness of the religious leaders and the people of God, He decided to communicate with each person on an individual level instead of communicating His instructions through a few chosen people, as He had done in the past. Each one of us who have approached the throne of God confessing our sins, accepted Jesus Christ, and been baptized, have the responsibility to learn to hear the voice of God, Christ, and the Holy Spirit. Without knowing the difference between your own voice and that which comes from God, we can never be sure we are not just talking to ourselves. We need to know that God is instructing and directing us and that we are not making things up based on our own plans and desires. Once we learn God's voice, we need to keep those things we receive sacred and not defile God's instructions with our own misguided desires and dreams. God does not need our help in deciding with what is needed. God formed His plan of salvation long before you and I were born. God needs us to carry out His instructions exactly the way we receive them. God is pouring His spirit upon us so that our spirit can be instructed and changed from within and not just from an external appearance. Those who are lost need preaching and teaching so they, too, can get connected and be instructed by God through our Lord Jesus Christ. God wants to instruct and teach us in the way we should go. He wants to counsel us so He can help us with our problems and troubles. Through this process, God can lead us into His plan of salvation through our Lord Jesus Christ. Because he instructs us through His great love and compassion, we who learn from God will instruct others in a gentle and kind way, as we were instructed. We have to be careful and guarded when we are instructed by God because there is great accountability to those whom He entrusts with Godly wisdom and knowledge. (Luke 12:47–48)

The Body of Christ

Another part of God's plan of salvation is the Body of Christ. God, knowing that we needed another way to live once we have become a new creation, prepared the Body of Christ not only to be a sacrifice, which had to go through death, but also to be a living body so we could have a body to be connected to once we put our body to death with our sinful nature. We now live because of Christ, who is on the inside of us. Though there are many different religions who believe in Christ, the Bible teaches us that there are different members of the Body of Christ and each member has a particular purpose. All the members are held together by the blood of Jesus. No part of the body should spend its time comparing itself to any other parts of the body to determine who's important, because all parts of the body are important to God the Father and our Lord Jesus Christ. Because we are a part of the Body of Christ, we must be very careful how we treat any other part of the Body of Christ. We cannot take an important part of the body (you) and defile it with this world or anything that does not build up the Body of Christ. One important thing that the Body of Christ provides is the removal of any differences in God's people. There is no difference between Jews and Gentiles. There is no difference between Blacks and Whites. There is no difference between Whites and Hispanics, and there is no difference between Blacks and Hispanics. There is no difference between the rich and the poor in the Body of Christ. There is no difference in those who love God, because we are all covered in the Body of Christ. There is one body, one race, one nation, all contained in the Body of Christ. You and I live together in the Body of Christ as brothers and sisters, children of God. We have been reconciled to God by our Lord Jesus Christ. Through the death and life of Jesus Christ, we can experience oneness with God.

> - *Ephesians 2:14–16 (NLT)*—"For Christ himself has brought peace to us. He united Jews and Gentiles into one people when, in his own body on the cross, he broke down the wall of hostility that separated us. He did this by ending the system of law with its commandments and regulations. He made peace between Jews and Gentiles by creating in himself one new people from the two groups. Together as one body, Christ reconciled both groups to God by means of his death on the cross, and our hostility toward each other was put to death."

The Assignment

Now that we are reconciled in the Body of Christ, we are being fitted for service. There are two interesting things about being assigned to perform God's work. I have come to learn that God will assign us our allotment based on the way we live. In the book of Jeremiah, God stated that He has assigned their allotment because they had forgotten the Lord and started turning to other things. When we are ready, God will assign us to the vineyard and field He wants us to care for. We do not get to pick where we are going to work for God; He decides based on His plan of salvation. It's very important that we listen to the teachings of Paul, once we reach this level of maturity. Once we are given an assignment by God, our lives become worthless and useless for any other purpose. We become totally committed to God the Father and our Lord Jesus Christ so we can be used to complete the assignment given to us by him. We are warned that we have to be very careful in the way we treat and interact with those God has chosen to give us to care for. We must work quickly to carry out the work that we have been assigned. There is impact and consequences in not completing God's work in a timely manner because we are an extension to God's plan of salvation for His people. We must work in the light while there is still time. One day, there will be no more time to work because God's plan of salvation is coming to end.

> *- John 9:4–5 (NLT)—"We must quickly carry out the tasks assigned us by the one who sent us. The night is coming, and then no one can work. But while I am here in the world, I am the light of the world."*

God the Father and our Lord Jesus Christ are hard at work preparing those who surrender their lives so they can become a worker in God's vineyard. God is also working to keep those who have been chosen on the path they were placed. Straying away from God's plan will cause God to change our assignment, either because we need to be retrained or our assignment is being taken away from us. God and Christ are at work preparing for the day when God will announce that the Day of Judgment has come and the door is shut. We who are called to work in God's vineyard must work quickly and be hard at work to impact all those who are lost and encourage those who are a part of the Body of Christ to move forward into full maturity. If we do this, those found in Christ will grow in confidence. Those who have worked in God's vineyard faithfully will receive a great reward for all their labor in God's truths.

God's Plan in the End

Death: As mentioned earlier, we all must come to a time in our lives where we must die. I used to believe that, in the beginning, God created us to live forever, but after examining this closer and listening to God's teaching, I have learned that was never a part of God's plan of salvation. The oldest person in the Old Testament lived until they were about a thousand years old. While this is a very long time to live, it was not eternity. Another important ingredient to eternal life is the purpose of the tree of life that was placed in the Garden of Eden; this is the source to receive eternal life. If we all must die, does it matter how or when we die? Is there anything to look forward to regarding the death process that can give us hope and peace? Actually, there is. God, knowing that we must all die, puts a promise in place to help comfort us when we approach our time of departure. He promised that, if we are found in Him, we will die peacefully. It does not promise that we will die a certain way but that we will die in peace. Another promise is those who follow godly paths will rest in peace when they die. Not only will we die in peace, but we will rest in peace until the Day of Judgment. Many of us are concerned about the timing of our death. As I continued to listen to God's voice and read His word, I have been taught that those who work in God's vineyard come to know when their assignment has come to an end and when it's time to rest from all of our labor. While there are many examples in the Bible that we can refer to, Paul's life is a good example of this process. He writes a letter to Timothy about having completed his assignment or the race. Paul speaks of pressing on to ensure he will receive the prize that he has worked so hard to achieve. He warns us not to run our race in vain. Jesus Christ also knew when his time on earth was coming to an end. If we live our lives to accomplish God's plan and accept our assignment and work to stay on God's path to assist in His plan of salvation, then you and I can have confidence that we will not die before our assignment is completed. Our bodies must experience death so our souls can experience the full salvation of God. Thank God we no longer have to wonder or live in fear. (Jeremiah 34:4–5), (Isaiah 57:2)

> *- 2 Timothy 4:6–8 (NLT)—"As for me, my life has already been poured out as an offering to God. The time of my death is near. I have fought the good fight, I have finished the race, and I have remained faithful. And now the prize awaits me—the crown of righteousness, which the Lord, the righteous Judge, will give me on the day of his return."*

God's Plan from the Beginning

Judgment: Much like death, we all must go through judgment. There are two components to the Final Judgment; one that rewards and another that condemns. We all must stand before the judgment seat of Christ, for judgment begins with the house of God. In the book of John, we are taught that if we believe in Christ and are part of the Body of Christ, there will be no judgment against us. This should give us confidence that we will be able to pass through judgment and into eternal life. If we continue to live a life of sin and evil, then we cannot have any confidence that we can make it through judgment. If we continue to disobey the Word of God and Christ Jesus, we will experience the anger of God. Christ tells us that the judgment he plans to carry out will be based on the righteous wisdom of God the Father. Jesus also shares that one of the reasons he came to earth was in preparation for judging the world. Christ warns us that anyone who rejects him or the message of the Good News will be judged by the truth they rejected. Again, much like many in the Old Testament experienced, a day of God's anger is coming; it's called the Day of Judgment. On Judgment Day, Christ will use fire to determine if our deeds can pass the test. While we may be saved, any works that do not survive will be burned up and the builder will suffer great loss. We who are confident should work hard to help snatch those who are destined for destruction out of the fire. Those who have lived rich lives and hoarded wealth will be eaten away by the flames of judgment and the heat of the fire. The very treasures that we have stored up will be evidence against us on Judgment Day. We should take this process very seriously. If God did not spare the angels who sinned and threw them into hell where there is gloomy darkness until the Day of Judgment, he will be especially hard on those who follow their own twisted sexual desires and who despise authority. We must believe that God knows how to rescue the godly people from their trials, even while holding the wicked for Judgment Day. We have been taught that the Day of Judgment will come like a thief in the night. We must stay ready and continue to work all the way until the end. How horrible and terrible the Day of Judgment will be for those who did not place their trust in God the Father and our Lord Jesus Christ. Thank God for His love and the love of our Lord Jesus Christ. (John 3:18–19), (Romans 14:10)

God's Plan from the Beginning

- 1 Peter 4:16–17 (NLT)—"But it is no shame to suffer for being a Christian. Praise God for the privilege of being called by his name! For the time has come for judgment, and it must begin with God's household. And if judgment begins with us, what terrible fate awaits those who have never obeyed God's Good News?"

Lake of Fire: We know that Judgment is coming even for those who have died. We all will stand before God's throne. It won't be a matter of what type of life you have lived, rich or poor; we all will get a chance to stand before Him. We know that the Devil's days are already numbered, for he will be thrown into he fiery lake of burning sulfur, joining the beast and the false prophet. There are those who will be a part of the first resurrection who will judge with Christ for a thousand years, and they will have no part of the second resurrection, for they were made to be priests for God and our Lord Jesus Christ. After a thousand years, Satan will be set free to deceive the nations on earth. Then, Christ will gather his army together for the great battle, and after Christ has defeated his enemies, the final judgment will come. Those who are raised in the second resurrection will be judged, and those who lie in graves and in the sea will stand and the Book of Life will be read. All will be judged according to what they have done, as recorded in the books. The lake of fire is the second death, where anyone whose name is not found recorded in the Book of Life will be thrown in, where there will be much pain and suffering. This will not be a good day for those who have not accepted Christ and surrendered their whole life over to him. If we are going to Church and pretending to live a godly life, pretending to love others or acting as if we are not selfish, our deeds will prove what is really in our hearts. It will be determined if we were just fooling ourselves the whole time. We may be able to fool those who cannot see what is hidden in us, but we won't be able to hide anything from Christ. Everything we have ever done will be seen by God. If we truly repent and allow the Holy Spirit to transform our lives, we have a chance to make it. God will ignore all the religious acts we have performed if we are not in Christ completely. Just becoming a part of Christ is not enough. We must seek to live in the full measure of the Body of

Christ so we can have confidence on that tragic last day. (Revelation 20:11–15)

New Heaven and Earth: From the creation of heaven and earth, God has desired to have a place that is not defiled and where His people can worship Him. Just as in the beginning, when God made a perfect place for man and woman to exist, He plans to remove all that is defiled and replace it with that which is holy to Him. God will once again replenish heaven and earth to make it fit for God's people. We know that God does not live on earth and that He makes heaven His home and earth His footstool. Just as He walked with Adam and Eve, God will once again walk with those who make it through judgment and are blessed with the privilege to live on a new earth. We can trust in God the Father and our Lord Jesus Christ that what has been prophesied will come to past. There will be a new heaven and earth as promised. And the glory of God and His righteousness will inhabit those who live on the earth. There will be a time after Judgment Day when God will actually make the old heaven and earth disappear. Can you imagine this great power of God, where even the sea will disappear? We need to be ready to pass through Judgment Day successfully so we can experience the regeneration of God's paradise on earth. We need to be confident that all the work we have done on earth will entitle us to experience the great wonder of God's power. No more will we experience destruction and waste as we experience it on earth today. There will be no more disease and sickness; we won't even experience the pain of death. It will be a great day when the world is once again inhabited by the presence of God; this will be a time of pure worship. (2 Peter 3:13)

> - *Revelation 21:1 (NLT)—"Then I saw a new heaven and a new earth, for the old heaven and the old earth had disappeared. And the sea was also gone."*

New Jerusalem: We know how much God loved Jerusalem, and He still plans to have Jerusalem as a special place of worship. Jerusalem's history is where many of the teachings of God originated. David lived in the town of Jerusalem. Even after sending His people to Babylon for punishment, God had them return and rebuild Jerusalem as a place of worship. We understand the importance of Jerusalem because it's the birth place of Jesus Christ and it's the same place where he suffered and was betrayed. Jesus Christ even grieved for Jerusalem because they killed so many of God's prophets who lived there. Many of the religious leaders came from Jerusalem. It was also the town where the Passover was celebrated. Jerusalem was the town that Satan offered when he tried to get Jesus Christ to bow down and worship him. It was in Jerusalem that God put His spirit in the disciples after Jesus was crucified. It was in Jerusalem where the Apostles and the head elders resided. It was in Jerusalem where God placed his cornerstone. Jerusalem was a place of great honor. And Jerusalem will be the place where Christ's judgment will take place. After that, God will create a New Jerusalem that will come down from heaven, and in it will be the temple of God. The temple will have gates of pearls, and the streets will be made of gold as clear as glass. The New Jerusalem will be prepared for the wedding day of Christ, it will be so wonderful to see, we need to get ready and remain prepared for going through judgment. We need to work so we can live with Christ in the New Jerusalem. (Revelation 3:11–12)

> *- Revelation 21:2 (NLT)—"And I saw the holy city, the new Jerusalem, coming down from God out of heaven like a bride beautifully dressed for her husband."*

Christ's Wedding: It is a part of God's plan to have a wedding for the joining together of the new heaven and earth with Jesus Christ. Our goal is to be a part of the wedding and do all that we can to get invited so we can rejoice with our Christ. We have to work so that we don't fall into the trap as described in the book of Matthew. When the wedding was announced, they were not willing to go but went their own way and ignored the call. We must be dressed and ready for service and keep our lamps burning, which is the fire inside of us. When the door is opened and Jesus arrives, we want to be one of the ones invited in. Those servants who are ready and waiting for his return will be rewarded. Jesus also teaches us how to act at the coming wedding when he stated that we should not sit in the seat of honor but wait on the host to come

God's Plan from the Beginning

and give us a seat of honor. God is busy preparing us for the coming wedding, and He is busy placing everything under the feet of Christ. (Revelation 19:7–9)

God's plan is the same now as it was in the beginning. As Jesus Christ stated, he and the Father are hard at work continuing to save souls who put their faith, trust, and hope in God the Father and our Lord Jesus Christ. God is also working to reveal and teach His wisdom and ways to those who work to become one with Christ and God the Father. Our goal should be to get our personal life in line with God's plan. We have to be transformed into the image of Jesus Christ, and we should be willing to surrender all our being, desires, and purpose to that which pleases God. We cannot hold on to our plans and partake of God's plan too. Jesus teaches us that if we want to gain the kingdom of God, we have to be willing to give up our lives. (Mark 8:37–37)

We know that God's plan is about saving souls, and it is not about getting rich, gaining materialistic items, or loving the things in this world. For us to be a part of God's plan, we have to be willing to separate from this world and all the things that bind us to it. We must learn to live in the Body of Christ so we are confident that we are a part of God's plan. God's plan is for those who love and trust in God the Father and our Lord Jesus Christ.

We are to seek and desire God's plan of salvation for ourselves, for our family, for our friends, for our co-workers, for our brothers and sisters in Christ, and for our enemies. Just like God the Father and our Lord Jesus Christ, we want everyone to be saved and experience the full plan of God's salvation. Amen.

God's Plan

The purpose of the following chart is to provide a visual understanding of the content in this chapter. The reader can use this chart to help deepen their understanding of God's Plan of Salvation. It describes how many of us are when we first come to Christ and how we sometime progress as we mature in Christ Jesus. There are scriptures to provide biblical support as the reader examines their life and where they are in Christ. The goal is to provide a tool that a believer would use many times as we struggle with life challenges and their sinful nature. We hope this tool helps bring the reader closer to God the Father and our Lord Jesus Christ. We all need to clearly understand where we are in our walk with Jesus Christ, and what we need to focus on to become more like Jesus Christ. We pray that this material will inspire you to continue in your walk of faith in the truth that comes from God.

God's Plan from the Beginning

God's Plan

We start out living outside the Will of God

God's Plans | **Our Plans** | **Our Desires**

We may have heard of God the Father or Jesus Christ, but we have no interest in knowing Him

God's Kingdom

We have not yet come to a point in our life where there is a need to cry out to God

We are taught about Jesus Christ, we accept Jesus Christ, we are baptized, receive the Holy Spirit. We are now on the road to salvation

God's Plans | **Our Plans** | **Our Desires**

We still try to carry out our desires and plans, only focusing on God sometimes

We are taught the truth about God. Depending on the teaching, we may become religious.

We start to know about God, but we are not in love with God the Father and Jesus Christ

God's Kingdom | Our Desires

1 Chron 28:9-10 (NLT) - 9 "And Solomon, my son, learn to know the God of your ancestors intimately. Worship and serve him with your whole heart and a willing mind. For the Lord sees every heart and knows every plan and thought. If you seek him, you will find him. But if you forsake him, he will reject you forever. 10 So take this seriously.

Prov 16:2-4 (NLT) - 2 People may be pure in their own eyes, but the Lord examines their motives. 3 Commit your actions to the Lord, and your plans will succeed. 4 The Lord has made everything for his own purposes, even the wicked for a day of disaster.

Isaiah 30:1-2 (NLT) - 1 "What sorrow awaits my rebellious children," says the Lord. "You make plans that are contrary to mine. You make alliances not directed by my Spirit, thus piling up your sins. 2 For without consulting me, you have gone down to Egypt for help.

2 Cor 1:17-19 (NLT) - 17 You may be asking why I changed my plan. Do you think I make my plans carelessly? Do you think I am like people of the world who say "Yes" when they really mean "No"? 18 As surely as God is faithful, my word to you does not waver between "Yes" and "No." 19 For Jesus Christ, the Son of God, does not waver between "Yes" and "No."

Jer 29:10-14 (NIV) - 11 For I know the plans I have for you," declares the Lord, "plans to prosper you and not to harm you, plans to give you hope and a future. 12 Then you will call upon me and come and pray to me, and I will listen to you. 13 You will seek me and find me when you seek me with all your heart. 14 I will be found by you," declares the Lord

God's Plan from the Beginning

God's Plan

Jesus Christ through the Holy Spirit starts setting us apart from the world and our own plans. We start to learn how to put sin to death in our lives, but we still hold onto some of our sins

God's Plans
Our Plans

We are taught the truth about God, and how to become spiritual and not religious

We continue to transgress against the Father, Jesus Christ, and the Holy Spirit

We start to understand what it means to surrender to God

We start feeling God's presences in our lives, but we don't continue in His will

Our Desires
God's Kingdom

Amos 3:7 (NIV) - 7 Surely the Sovereign Lord does nothing without revealing his plan to his servants the prophets.

James 4:14-16 (NLT) - 14 How do you know what your life will be like tomorrow? Your life is like the morning fog—it's here a little while, then it's gone.15 What you ought to say is, "If the Lord wants us to, we will live and do this or that." 16 Otherwise you are boasting about your own plans, and all such boasting is evil.

Jesus Christ is able to use us and send us out to spread the Good News, but the work is not complete in us, we still need to continue seeking God as we grow and mature in his knowledge

God's Plans
Our Plans

We know what it means to be in love with God the Father and Jesus Christ

The Holy Spirit is working strong in us, and we are in close fellowship with Christ

We are on the path of totally surrendering to God the Father and Jesus Christ

We desire and seek to walk in God's presence the whole day, nothing is more important

We look to walk with God all during the day, all our desires and dreams are focused on him

God's Kingdom
Our Desires

Eph 1:11 (NIV) - 11 In him we were also chosen, having been predestined according to the plan of him who works out everything in conformity with the purpose of his will

Isaiah 30:1-2 (NLT) - 1 "What sorrow awaits my rebellious children," says the Lord. "You make plans that are contrary to mine. You make alliances not directed by my Spirit, thus piling up your sins. 2 For without consulting me, you have gone down to Egypt for help.

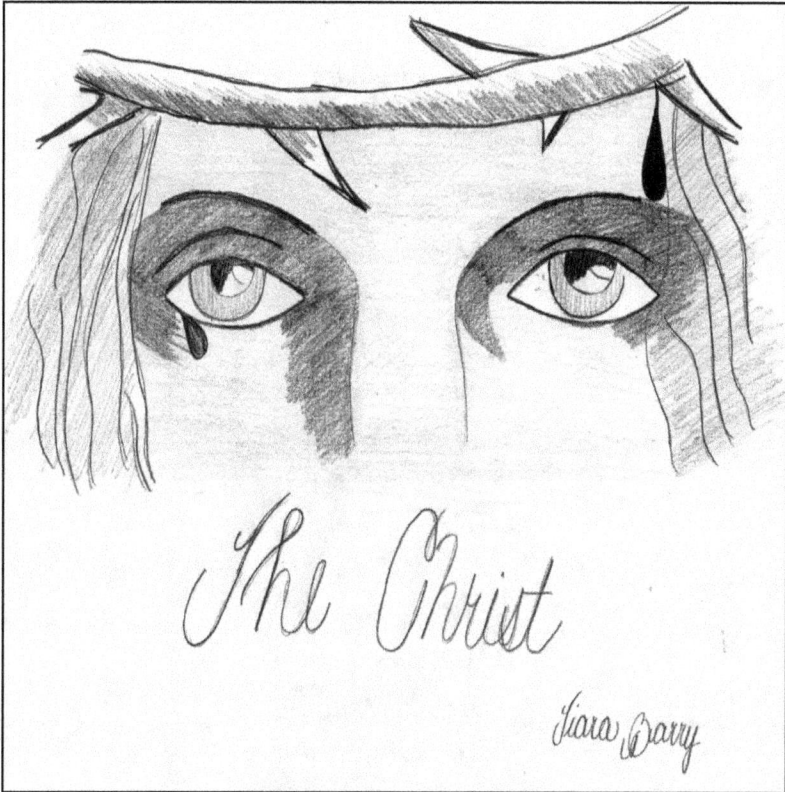

The Christt

Tiara Barry

The Christ

Chapter 2

HE and I

by Donna Maria Barry

HE envisioned

HE foreseen

HE decided

HE spoke

I am the creation of GOD

HE designed

HE customized

HE constructed

HE completed

I am the creation of GOD

HE was excited

HE was compassionate

HE was creative

HE was pleased

I am the creation of GOD

HE is FATHER..........GOD

I am his likeness

HE is CREATOR.........MASTER

I am his servant

HE and I........have an Exclusive Relationship

The Christ

Introduction

A lot of controversy surrounds who Jesus Christ really is and His purpose. We will review Jesus Christ's position, role, authority, purpose, and His priesthood. The purpose is to give us full confidence that we can truly depend on Jesus Christ to fulfill that which God the Father has empowered him to do—that is, to make a way for the lost, to save those who receive him, to instruct those who are called, to execute judgment, and to lead us into the Kingdom of God. Once we are joined together with Jesus Christ by us accepting and believing in him, we are encouraged to walk by the very faith we exercised when we became born again, as we grow in Christ. There are three important take-a-ways: We must believe in the Son of God (Jesus Christ), we must increase our faith, and we must always exercise our faith as we work and live through circumstances and situations.

The Establishment of Christ

Who is Jesus Christ? Is He the Father in the flesh? Is He God? Is He the Son of God? Is He an angel? Did He exist before coming to earth? These are all valid questions, and scripture gives us the answers we are seeking. Why is this important? It's important for several reasons, which we will further examine. But the most important reason is so you and I will know how to approach God the Father, in whom we can place our trust and faith in to lead us. So where do we begin? Let's start at the beginning and work our way through the Bible to get a holistic picture of Jesus Christ. First, there were the prophets who predicted the coming of Jesus Christ. (Isaiah 7:14), (Isaiah 9:6–7)

It wasn't until God shared more information with us that we learned that Jesus Christ existed from the beginning. In the book of Proverbs, Chapter 8, Jesus Christ's birth is described to us. The scripture describes the point when God the Father formed him, before anything else was created. The scripture goes on to share with us that he was appointed in past ages, before the earth was created. It goes on to say that he was there when God the Father established the heavens and he was the architect at God the Father's side. In John 1:1, we learn that, in the beginning, Christ was with God, He was God and God the Father created everything through him and nothing existed that was not created by Jesus Christ. And in verse 11, we see that Jesus Christ became human and was full of love and faithfulness. And we have seen his glory; the glory of the Father's one and only Son. As I ponder the position of God, I prayed for more clarity. I was taught that we should see the use of the word God as a title. (John 10:34–36)

We know that Jesus Christ is not God the Father. If he were God the Father, then we could not explain the things that He taught us. For one, Jesus tells us that everything He learned was taught to him by God the Father. (John 5:30)

> - John 5:36—"But I have a greater witness than John—my teachings and my miracles. The Father gave me these works to accomplish, and they prove that he sent me. And the Father who sent me has testified about me himself. You have never heard his voice or seen him face to face, and you do not have his message in your hearts, because you do not believe me—the one he sent to you."

Also in Colossians, Paul shares a very powerful description of Christ.

> -Colossians 1:15–20—"Christ is the visible image of the invisible God. He existed before anything was created and is supreme over all creation, for through him God created everything in the heavenly realms and on earth. He made the things we can see and the things we can't see—such as thrones, kingdoms, rulers, and authorities in the unseen world. Everything was created through him and for him. He existed before anything else, and he holds all creation together. Christ is also the head of the church, which is his body. He is the beginning, supreme over all who rise from the dead. So he is first in everything. For God in all his fullness was pleased to live in Christ, and through him God reconciled everything to himself. He made peace with everything in heaven and on earth by means of Christ's blood on the cross."

The Christ

There are many more scriptures that support Jesus Christ being prepared by God the Father to save and lead us. He was not only prepared to save us, but to also become our God. We now have God the Father and our Lord God, Jesus Christ. The timing of when God the Father appointed Jesus as God over us is unclear in the scriptures. However, there are scriptures that let us know Christ's promotion did occur. In Hebrews 1:8–9, God the Father speaks to Jesus Christ as God, in stating "God, your God." It goes on to describe this promotion and sets the order of who reports to Him. Even the angels are made to worship the Christ. Let me share something interesting about this timing. If you go back and look at the Old Testament, there is reference to this promotion. (Psalms 45:6–7)

This should bring up a lot of questions, depending on your religious background and training. We have to come to the understanding that the only way to God the Father is through Jesus Christ; there is no other way. God the Father is revealed to us through the Son. (Luke 10:22)

God the Father goes through a process to put Jesus Christ in the anointed role that was defined from the beginning of time. Then there is the question of what was Jesus before God the Father anointed him as our God?

If you read Hebrews 1:9, a comparison is made between Jesus Christ and the angels. It states that Jesus Christ was set above his companions, which makes me believe he had to be either an angel or considered on the same level as an angel. Either way, God the Father separated Jesus from the angels and anointed Him as our God. Let's look at how God placed everything under Jesus Christ. (Ephesians 1:9–11)

God Places Everything under Jesus Christ

To start, God the Father created the world you and I live in through Jesus Christ, and Christ gave life to everything that was created (John 1:1–15). The Bible teaches in Isaiah 11:10, "In that day the heir to David's throne will be a banner of salvation to all the world. The nations will rally to him, and the land where he lives will be a glorious place". Personally, I believe that there are times in the Old Testament where the prophets and religious leaders were actually speaking to Jesus Christ and not just to the Father. It doesn't seem to make any sense that God the Father would have used Jesus Christ just to create the world and then take over and do all the speaking and teaching. Just a point of thought: We know that God's ways are higher than ours. God is at work, establishing and putting things into place for Christ. (Luke 20:42–43)

We know that God had a plan from the beginning, and He is executing His divine plan. God the Father placed Jesus Christ in his place of authority to care for, love, comfort, and to judge the world.

Jesus Christ the High Priest

A part of God's plan was for Jesus Christ to become the High Priest for all believers. We know that God calls individuals into priestly service. The same was true with Jesus Christ. Hebrews 5:1–6 describes the selection process. Verse five reads "Christ also did not take upon himself the glory of becoming a high priest, but God said to him, 'you are a priest forever, in the order of Melchizedek." The Priest must be called of God, even as Aaron was. It is an honor that no man takes for himself. No one elects himself. It would be presumptions for any individual to claim Priesthood for himself without first being called and appointed. As a part of God's covenant with man, He requires a sacrifice for the forgiveness and removal of sin. In the Old Testament, God accepted sacrifices by the high priests. The Priest had to first cleanse himself and then make a sacrifice for the sins of man each and every year. This allowed us to remain in God's grace and favor and to be accepted by God and receive His blessings. Toward the end of the Old Testament, the priests had become greedy and were performing their priestly duties for money and the people of God stopped obeying the Word of God. (Malachi 2:5–9)

So God the Father decided to create a new covenant. He needed a High Priest who would not be corrupted by the world and its desires. So God the Father anointed Jesus Christ as High Priest to carry out his will that was declared from the beginning of the world. Jesus Christ as the new High Priest, allows God the Father to show us mercy and grace through His Son. (Hebrews 7:26–28)

So with the change of priesthood, we all can come to the throne of God, knowing that there is no corruption, greed, or sin in the High Priest we serve. Now, let's take a look at what Jesus Christ had to do to take his place on the throne of God and become our God.

Jesus Christ Completes his Mission on Earth

In Hebrews 2:5–18, we see that Jesus Christ had a mission that was given to him by God the Father. He gave up his position and became lower than the angels. He had to suffer death, to conquer death. He made our salvation perfect through his suffering. He declared the name of God the Father to those he called brother. He shared in our humanity to overcome the devil. He freed us who feared death. He became like us so he could be a merciful and faithful High Priest to us. He made atonement for our sins with his blood; he suffered, and was tempted he is able to help we who are being tempted. Then, Jesus Christ sat down at the right hand of God the Father to take his position on the throne of God. Jesus, while carrying out his mission, had times when he questioned if he should complete the assignment or even care enough to love us as his own. In Luke 9:41, Jesus makes a comment as he continues the mission. (Luke 9:41)

Because he gave up his position and took on the flesh of man, Jesus knows how hard it is to make it and stay focused on God's will. Jesus understands as we struggle with the flesh, our desire to be in control, and all the evil desires that control our minds and bodies. He went back up to heaven to present himself to the Father, and there was a great celebration in heaven as Jesus stood before the throne. (Revelation 5:11–13)

So Christ was received up into heaven and there was great rejoicing, for Christ had completed his mission on earth. Now we see Jesus in heaven preparing the army of God for battle, still wearing the robe soaked in blood. (Revelation 19:12–16)

We have to understand that Jesus Christ and God the Father is always at work, preparing for the completion of God's plan.

Jesus Christ Has the Authority and Power

Even before completing his mission on earth, Jesus Christ received power and authority from God the Father. As with any position, if it doesn't come with any authority or power, then it doesn't have the ability to have a large impact. Just imagine if Jesus Christ were not granted full authority and power, many would just consider him a priest, pastor, or a good person. But, with all authority and power, lives can be changed, and those who do not believe have a chance to believe. So Christ set out to prove to man that he had been given all authority and power.

Christ's Authority

Once Jesus Christ started his ministry on earth, he set out to demonstrate the authority of God. In Matthew 9:6, Jesus makes a statement that he plans to prove to us he has authority. (Matthew 9:6)

Jesus Christ then lets us know that he has been given not just some of the authority to rule, but that God the Father gave him all the authority to do His will.(Matthew 28:18)

It was and is essential that we understand and give reverence to the authority of Jesus Christ. The good thing regarding authority is, if you have all authority, you can delegate it to others. Jesus Christ chose 12 individuals to delegate his authority to.

- Matthew 10:1—"Jesus called his twelve disciples together and gave them authority to cast out evil spirits and to heal every kind of disease and illness."

Even today, if we choose to give up our desires and will, as Jesus Christ did, we can walk in the authority of God and our Lord Jesus Christ. (Colossians 2:9–10)

Knowing that Jesus Christ has all the authority to take care of us, we should be open to living under his leadership and direction, even if that means giving up our own lives to accomplish God's will.

Christ's Power

In addition to receiving all authority, Jesus Christ was given the power of God to execute his authority. Like with any power and authority, it can be used to teach, instruct, guide, influence, correct, judge, and punish. Jesus Christ has a place on God's throne, and he is seated with great power and authority. (Matthew 26:64)

A person with all power can delegate their power to others. Jesus Christ did a marvelous thing when he granted his authority to his Apostles (Disciples), including the power to execute God's will. (Luke 9:1)

The mechanism put in place for us to receive power from God and our Lord Jesus Christ is the Holy Spirit.

- Acts 1:7–8—"He replied, 'The Father alone has the authority to set those dates and times, and they are not for you to know. But you will receive power when the Holy Spirit comes upon you. And you will be my witnesses, telling people about me everywhere—in Jerusalem, throughout Judea, in Samaria, and to the ends of the earth."

The Christ

We know that receiving the Holy Spirit is not something we can study to receive, purchase, claim, or obtain by following religious rituals or teachings. It is given freely to those who truly love God, trust God, and seek to do God's will. (1 Corinthians 2:4–5)

The power of God and our Lord Jesus Christ is released through the Holy Spirit. It reveals and searches our thoughts to correct us, and it communicates with our spirit to teach us by which authority and power we should operate to do God's will, as stated in 1 Corinthians 2:10–12—*"But it was to us that God revealed these things by his Spirit. For his Spirit searches out everything and shows us God's deep secrets. No one can know a person's thoughts except that person's own spirit, and no one can know God's thoughts except God's own Spirit. And we have received God's Spirit (not the world's spirit), so we can know the wonderful things God has freely given us."*

The Bible opens our eyes to the power and authority granted to Jesus Christ and how faithful he is with what God the Father has entrusted him with, our very lives. We also have a part to play. We must not only believe in the authority and power of Jesus Christ, but we must also now walk in the faith that comes with this great understanding and hope. Finally, in the book of Revelation, Jesus gave us his guarantee of his 2nd coming. *(Revelation 22:12–20)*

We have a promise from our Lord Jesus Christ that he will return and reward us for our suffering for the Kingdom of God and for believing in the one and only Son of God. Amen.

Prayer to the Lord

Lord Jesus, we come to you because you are our God.
We come to praise and give you honor, for you are worthy.
We thank God the Father for sending you.
We thank you for the love you continue to show us.
We thank you for paying the high price for our salvation.
We thank you for sending the Holy Spirit to prepare us.
We praise you for what you continue to do for us.
We praise you for always forgiving our sins.
We praise you for the peace that surpasses all understanding.
We praise you for the joy and comfort that you provide for us.
We praise you for being our savior and granting us grace.
We worship you for who you are.
We worship you because you are the alpha and the omega.
We worship you because you are worthy to sit on the throne of God.
We worship you because all things were created for you and by you.
We worship you because all that you do pleases the Father.
We worship you because you shed your blood for us.
We worship because you are Lord God over all our lives.
We give you all the glory because it's the least we can do.
We give you all the glory; because all things come through you.
We give you all the glory because it pleases the Father.
We give you all the glory because you have been anointed King of Kings.
We give you all the glory because you are our High Priest.
We give you all the glory because you saved a wretch like me.
We give you all the glory because of who you are.
We give you all the glory, all authority and power is in your hands.
Thank you for taking on all our pain and suffering.
Thank you for making a way out of no way.
Thank you for being a light in a dark world.
Thank you for showing us mercy when we did not deserve it.
Thank you for continuing to cover us as we grow in our faith.
Thank you for protecting our mind, body, and soul from destruction.
Thank you for blessing us and storing up our reward in heaven.
Thank you for keeping our family safe and out of harm's way.
You are worthy; you are worth all our praise and worship.
We thank God the Father for you. Amen.

To Know God for Yourself

The purpose of the chart is to provide a visual understanding of the content in this chapter. The reader can use this chart to help evaluate where they are in connecting to Christ. So many of us have remained connected to Christ through our religious organizations, but we have not developed a personal relationship with Christ. As you continue to study and grow, use this chart to help support your calling in the Body of Christ. If you are called to be a church leader, use this chart to help bring the people God entrust into your care to a right relationship with Christ so we all will experience God's salvation through our Lord Jesus Christ to the glory of God the Father.

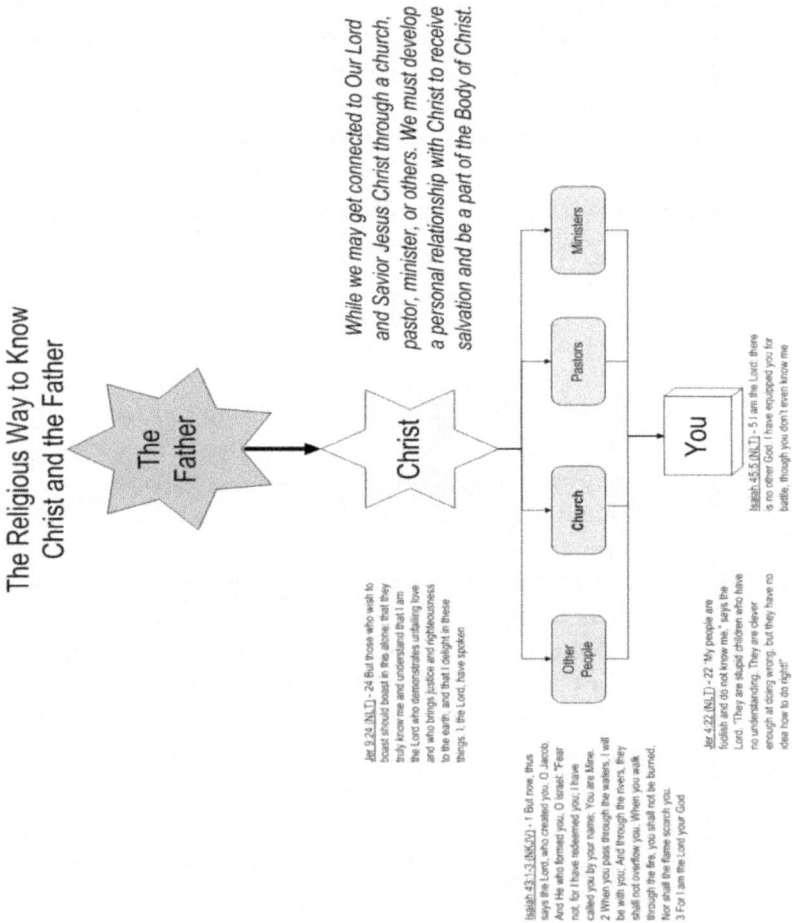

The Religious Way to Know Christ and the Father

While we may get connected to Our Lord and Savior Jesus Christ through a church, pastor, minister, or others. We must develop a personal relationship with Christ to receive salvation and be a part of the Body of Christ.

The Father → Christ → Other People / Church / Pastors / Ministers → You

Jer 9:24 (NLT) - 24 But those who wish to boast should boast in this alone: that they truly know me and understand that I am the Lord who demonstrates unfailing love and who brings justice and righteousness to the earth, and that I delight in these things. I, the Lord, have spoken

Isaiah 43:1-3 (NKJV) - 1 But now, thus says the Lord, who created you, O Jacob, And He who formed you, O Israel: "Fear not, for I have redeemed you; I have called you by your name; You are Mine. 2 When you pass through the waters, I will be with you; And through the rivers, they shall not overflow you. When you walk through the fire, you shall not be burned, Nor shall the flame scorch you. 3 For I am the Lord your God

Jer 4:22 (NLT) -22 "My people are foolish and do not know me," says the Lord. "They are stupid children who have no understanding. They are clever enough at doing wrong, but they have no idea how to do right!"

Isaiah 45:5 (NLT) - 5 I am the Lord; there is no other God. I have equipped you for battle, though you don't even know me

The Spiritual Way to Know Christ and the Father

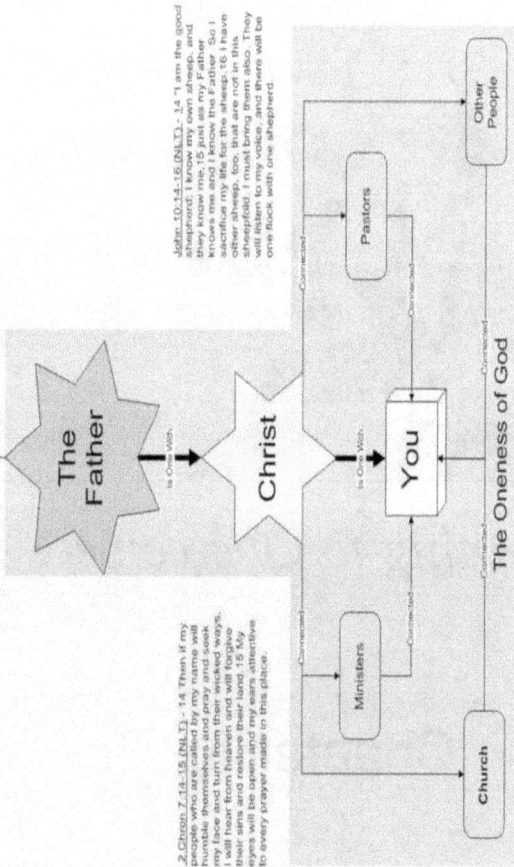

2 Chron 7:14-15 (NLT) - 14 Then if my people who are called by my name will humble themselves and pray and seek my face and turn from their wicked ways, I will hear from heaven and will forgive their sins and restore their land. 15 My eyes will be open and my ears attentive to every prayer made in this place.

John 10:14-16 (NLT) - 14 "I am the good shepherd; I know my own sheep, and they know me. 15 just as my Father knows me and I know the Father. So I sacrifice my life for the sheep. 16 I have other sheep, too, that are not in this sheepfold. I must bring them also. They will listen to my voice, and there will be one flock with one shepherd.

Rev 3:5 (NLT) - 5 All who are victorious will be clothed in white. I will never erase their names from the Book of Life, but I will announce before my Father and his angels that they are mine

John 17:9-11 (NKJV) - 9 I pray for them. I do not pray for the world but for those whom You have given Me, for they are Yours. 10 And all Mine are Yours, and Yours are Mine, and I am glorified in them. 11 Now I am no longer in the world, but these are in the world, and I come to You. Holy Father, keep through Your name those whom You have given Me, that they may be one as We are.

The Father — Is One With → Christ — Is One With → You

Ministers, Pastors, Other People, Church — Connected

The Oneness of God

Heb 8:10-12 (NLT)

10 But this is the new covenant I will make with the people of Israel on that day, says the Lord: I will put my laws in their minds, and I will write them on their hearts. I will be their God, and they will be my people.

11 And they will not need to teach their neighbors, nor will they need to teach their relatives, saying, 'You should know the Lord.' For everyone, from the least to the greatest, will know me already.

12 And I will forgive their wickedness, and I will never again remember their sins

OVERCOMING THE WORLD...

Learning to Overcome

Chapter 3

GOD AND I CARE

By Donna Barry

When your heart is broken and suspended in air
There just might be times when I cannot be there
If you'll close your eyes and imagine my face
You'll see me praying that God grants you grace

In case you are thinking there's no way I can know
What *you* experience with your heart so low
In my ear God is whispering the things that you feel
And I will not abandon you as you mend and heal

Oh how I wish I had all the answers for you
Why is this happening and what should you do
And while you are searching for answers my friend
Please believe I am searching over here on my end

Day in and day out the whole day through
I ask God for strength so I can be there for you
There are going to be trials that you'll have to bear
But have faith in knowing that God and I care

Your days will be labeled some good some bad
There might even be days when you get really mad
And during those times when you won't want to talk
I am confident God's with you where ever you walk

There's absolutely nothing that compares to God's love
Not belonging to this world but it comes from above
Talk to him cry to him do whatever you must
He's standing there waiting just give him your trust

Learning to Overcome

Why are we overcome by life?

One of the most difficult things for a Christian to deal with and understand is all the trials and tribulations that continue to come our way. If I have given my life to Christ, why aren't things a lot better for me? Many religious teachings have God's people focusing on prosperity, but money does not solve all trials and tribulations. And in some situations, money is what causes these trials and tribulations. For example, we have read or heard of stories where a person who acquired riches or wealth struggled with issues such as immoral sexual sins, dishonest behavior, or debt issues. This is why Jesus teaches us not to focus on wealth as a means to overcome troubles in life. (Matthew 6:19–21)

So, if money is not the means by which God will help us overcome, then by what means will God provide? The answer to this question is found in a number of scriptures. First, we need to understand why we experience trials and tribulations in the first place. I believe the answer is pretty straightforward for most of us. Sin is what caused and is causing trials and tribulations to come into our lives. It could be sin that we invoke or sin being invoked by others whom we associate with. In Ezekiel, we are taught that two issues caused sin: the person that sees and knows the sin is happening but does nothing to prevent it, and the person who is committing the sin. However, if a person sees sin coming and does not warn others, they become guilty as well.

> *- Ezekiel 33:6 (NIV)—"But if the watchman sees the sword coming and does not blow the trumpet to warn the people and the sword comes and takes the life of one of them, that man will be taken away because of his sin, but I will hold the watchman accountable for his blood."*

Many times, we experience trials and tribulations because we either commit sin or we do nothing to prevent it from happening, so God holds both accountable. If we stop sinning or assist in helping others to stop sinning or we have nothing to do with sinners, the number of trials and tribulations we experience will be reduced. We can eliminate trials and tribulations that are caused by sinning when we stop sinning. Sounds easy, right? The other reason trials and tribulations come our way is because God is testing us. Unfortunately, when we confess our sins to God, He does not remove the trials and tribulations from our lives.

You see, God is interested in several things once we confess and are baptized:

1) God is concerned that we become aware of the sins contained in our body, mind, and soul. Yes, our sins were forgiven, but our body will need to be put under the control of God. These trials and tribulations come from a lack of self-control. (1 Peter 1:13–16)

2) God will also test where we are in our journey to overcome sin and how close we are in becoming like Christ. God teaches that we need to be transformed and changed into the image of Christ. So God uses trials and tribulations to teach us where we are in our transformation process, and what remains to complete the total change. (Romans 12:1–2)

The final reason we experience trials and tribulations is because God has deemed it necessary to complete His plan and will. Many times, in the Word of God, we see people who were born with a condition. Other times, a person was overcome with an ailment that changed their life. There are even times where God chose to end a person's life, even though they lived a Godly life. All of these situations and circumstances were driven by the will of God. He may have called someone to depart from this world and be with Him early in life. He could have planned for a person to know Him through a condition or to be shown Christ through healing. God's will could be that a person becomes a living testimony to save others. Most times, these conditions are not a result of sin, but there are conditions that come from sin. We need to gain an understanding from God so that the reason for the condition is made clear to us. Even through sickness, God can receive glory. (John 11:3–4)

Now that we know what causes trials and tribulations to come into our lives, we need to understand what we can do about these conditions. The good news is that Jesus Christ provides us a way out.

> *-1 Corinthians 10:13 (NIV)—"No temptation has seized you except what is common to man. And God is faithful; he will not let you be tempted beyond what you can bear. But when you are tempted, he will also provide a way out so that you can stand up under it."*

Overcome with Emotion: There are things in our lives that cause us to go through serious emotional trials. This may come from a death in the family, as David experienced or it could be from expectations that we have of God. (2 Samuel 18:33)

We know that the emotional trial that David experienced was from failing to keep God's Word, and committing sin. It's important to understand the reason why we are dealing with great emotional problems, because we need to understand how we must approach God to overcome them. Do we need to confess our transgressions or do we need to be praying for faith and deliverance?

Overcome with Misery: Many times, we experience misery because we get involved in the wrong situation or we use what God has provided for the wrong purpose. Misery comes from the fact that we knew better but decided our way was better than God's plan. When things don't work out, misery sets in as things become more difficult, and sometimes we have no choice but to give up everything. Job is a perfect example. He had everything, but he became self-righteous, so God decided to allow Satan to have his way. (Job 20:22)

> *- 1 John 1:9 (NIV)—"If we confess our sins, he is faithful and just and will forgive us our sins and purify us from all unrighteousness."*

Learning to Overcome

Overcome with Grief: Grief is an interesting thing to overcome because it does not come from our sins or from us experiencing misery. Grief comes from feeling the hurt and pain of others. Jeremiah was overcome with grief because his people were suffering from sickness and disease. (Jeremiah 8:21–22) (NLT)—"I hurt with the hurt of my people. I mourn and am overcome with grief. Is there no medicine in Gilead? Is there no physician there? Why is there no healing for the wounds of my people?" While God may have gifted some with the ability to heal, some healing can only come through prayer. Jesus taught this to his disciples.

> *- Mark 9:28–29 (NLT)—"Afterward, when Jesus was alone in the house with his disciples, they asked him, 'Why couldn't we cast out that evil spirit?' Jesus replied, 'This kind can be cast out only by prayer.'"*

Overcoming grief requires a group of praying and faithful people to be involved in the situation. We know the prayers of the righteous are heard by God.

> *- Proverbs 15:29 (NLT)—"The Lord is far from the wicked, but he hears the prayers of the righteous."*

Overcome with Evil: Many times, we spend a lot of our prayer time talking to God about what Satan is doing in our life, but the issue may be what we are allowing Satan to control in our lives. To overcome evil, we need to surrender our lives over to God and stop doing what we want to do. We need to allow God to order our steps so we can be taught about God's decrees and actually do God's will. (Psalms 119:133–135)

We have to understand that Satan can only have a foothold in our lives if we choose to allow it. If we depend on God, He will protect us so we can overcome evil. We must believe that the way to overcome evil is by always doing good.

> *- Romans 12:21 (NIV)—"Do not be overcome by evil, but overcome evil with good."*

Overcome with Addiction: Addiction is an area almost all of us have experienced, either directly or through a loved one. Either way, it affects not only the person under addiction but also those who love them. Overcoming addiction is not a getting-One self-well solution, though a person may be able to break the habit for a moment. Without being completely freed from the bondage, Satan will wait and use it against that person again. We have to believe that God wants us free from addiction so the life He gave is not ruined. The only way a person can get totally free from every form of addiction is by receiving the Holy Spirit. They need to learn God's will for their life and work to not separate from God. They need to be thankful for each day, praise and worship God, and be determined to live free from addiction. (Ephesians 5:17–20)

I have seen a person walk away from addiction, never to turn back. God's Holy Spirit can sweep this issue clean from a person's life, if they just believe, have faith, and stand firm.

Overcome with Anger: There are a number of reasons we need to overcome anger. First, we have to understand that anger is one of the Number One ways sin gets birthed in us. If we can control our anger, many of the sins we carry out would not occur. Secondly, allowing anger to exist gives the devil a foothold into our lives. We may be under control some days, but the devil can invoke a foothold he has on us at any time. And last, we have to understand that our anger has a lasting effect on those whom we are trying to encourage to give their lives to Christ. If people are looking at you as an example of a person being transformed into Christ's image, when they see you acting out anger, what happens to their faith? (Ephesians 4:26–27)

Overcome with Fear: Fear is one of those issues that, at first glance, one only thinks of the obvious things such as the fear of flying in a plane, fear of heights, or fear of getting hurt. But, if you are not a person who suffers from fear, you tend to take it lightly. However, there are people who have fears that prevent them from operating in a normal environment. They can become so overcome with fear that they can't leave the house. Then there is the fear of death. Some fear how they are going to die, yet others fear the fact we all will die. Sometimes, as in the book of Luke, we are so overwhelmed with fear that we cannot even pray or allow God to speak to us. (Luke 8:37)

Knowing how real fear can be, we need to find a way to get it removed from our lives. Unfortunately, we do not understand that fear is the opposite of love. So if we fear, then we have to acknowledge that the Love of God is not deep in us. (1 John 4:18)

The first step in overcoming fear is to get the love of God deep in our hearts, then God steps in and gives us a promise. He teaches us that we are not to fear anything man can do to us but, if we fear God, He will help us.

> - *Hebrews 13:6 (NLT)*—*"The Lord is my helper, so I will have no fear. What can mere people do to me?"*

We also know that God will not allow us to be tempted more than we can bear, and He will provide a way out for us. (1 Corinthians 10:13)

Overcoming fear requires that we stand on the promises of God, surrender to God's loving care, and give Him total control. Then watch God the Father and our Lord Jesus Christ at work.

Overcome with Dreams: I have meet many people who are haunted by their dreams. These individuals dream of being killed or Satan interacting with them or they experience murder and terror. While Daniel's gift of interpreting dreams seems wonderful, I don't think I would want to understand some people's dreams. (Daniel 4:19)

I believe, in our dreams, we experience the truth about our fears, wants, desires, and passions. When we are awake, we have some sense of control over our thinking, but when we are asleep, our thoughts turn to what is on the inside of us. King Nebuchadnezzar suffered from some troubled dreams. Though he had all the riches in the world, the things that entered his mind at night haunted him during the day. So how do we get our dreams to not consist of killing, Satan, dying, or terror?

The key is the Word of God. If you are a born-again Christian, the Holy Spirit lives inside you. But, for the Holy Spirit to operate effectively, it needs the Word of God planted deep inside of you. So, when bad dreams come upon you in your sleep, your spirit being connected to the Holy Spirit can speak the Word of God and protect your dreams. The other thing that aids in overcoming bad dreams is having a pure heart. One thing Satan cannot operate against is a pure heart filled with the Holy Spirit. (Hebrews 10:19–23)

The last thing that helps us overcome bad dreams is putting a song in our hearts about Christ. When our spirit sings a hymn about God and our Lord Jesus at night, it helps us to overcome. (Colossians 3:16–17)

We need to get the junk out of our ears, eyes, and mind. We need to let the Spirit of the Lord lead us night and day so we can have peace which surpasses all understanding.

Overcome with Unbelief: There is no way we can accomplish what God has directed us to do or utilize the gifts He has blessed us with if there is any unbelief in us. God's promises are based on us having a trusting relationship with Him. If we don't have complete trust in God, we cannot have complete confidence that what we achieved came from God. Just saying we believe in God and our Lord Jesus Christ is not enough.
   - Mark 9:24 (NLT)—"The father instantly cried out, 'I do believe, but help me overcome my unbelief!.'"

Many have demonstrated a form of faith, yet unbelief exists in other areas of their walk with God. We need to learn to overcome our unbelief. Many times, our unbelief comes when things are not going well with us. As long as things are running smoothly, we tend to show a lot of trust in God. But, let the wheel start coming off the wagon and see how much trust in God we display. God wants to know, in the middle of our troubles, are we willing to trust in Him still. When things get difficult, do we lean on our own understanding, creativity, ideas, and solutions or do we stand firm and fully persuaded that we trust God? One thing is for sure, we cannot put our trust in God if we are not willing to live in accordance to His ways. Placing our trust in God while continuing to enjoy our sinful desires and pleasures is foolish. God is not interested in appeasing our wants just for our sake. What glory is there in that for God? We overcome our unbelief by allowing God to teach us how to overcome this world. We must allow God to be in control of our lives and seek His face and direction in everything we do. We overcome our unbelief by demonstrating to God that nothing in this world matters but His will.

Overcome with Discouragement: Many times, we become discouraged because we have placed our faith in something that has failed us. Whether this feeling of discouragement is true or justified does not really matter because we feel the way we feel. Maybe we have placed our faith in a religious leader who did not or has not conducted themselves in a manner we accept or approve of, so we get discouraged. Maybe our spouse has not lived up to what we believe they should be, so we get discouraged. Maybe our children or family members are not living up to our expectations, so we get discouraged. There is one single common denominator in these situations: We had or have an expectation of another person that we believed was or is not being lived up to. Instead of putting our trust and expectations in God, we decided the best place to have our expectations is in another person. Placing our trust in someone who does not have or who is not in total control seems to be a misplacement of our trust. We must learn to place our trust in God so we can never be discouraged by the actions of another person. If someone does discourage us, we are in a great position to forgive them because we knew they were not in total control in the first place.

> - *2 Corinthians 2:7 (NLT)—"Now, however, it is time to forgive and comfort him. Otherwise he may be overcome by discouragement."*

We are in a great position to comfort the person who let us down and let them know that God has it under control. We overcome discouragement by trusting in God the Father and our Lord Jesus Christ and having a forgiving heart.

Learning to Overcome

Overcome with Desires: If we could learn to overcome our desires that go against God's will, this whole world would suddenly be a better place. For most people, the issue with desires is that they are self-focused and self-seeking. Even when we have desires to help others, an underlining self-seeking agenda is always in the midst. Our desires have us so wrapped up that we go to church praying that God will help us achieve our own personal desires. Our desire to be right causes us to fight until we get our way. Our desire to be loved causes us to seek love in all types of relationships. Our desire to be rich causes us to seek financial wealth no matter what the cost. Our desires keep us blinded, confused, and wanting more and more. When we fail to achieve our desires, we blame it all on others. (James 4:1–3)

Overcoming our evil desires requires for us to change our motives. We cannot change our motives without a change of heart. We cannot change our heart without the Holy Spirit. We cannot experience the Holy Spirit without Christ.

Overcome with Darkness: How do we overcome something that is so deep into our soul that we would be a different person without it? We all have some things in our lives that are very hard to get rid of, even for a born-again Christian. These things are hidden, and we don't talk about them. We just carry them out. Even though we go to church every week and pay our tithes, these things are still present in us. They are the dark side of ourselves that we try to hide, but practicing religion will not get these things removed.

> *- Matthew 6:23 (NLT)—"But when your eye is bad, your whole body is filled with darkness. And if the light you think you have is actually darkness, how deep that darkness is!"*

To overcome darkness, we have to get to a place where we are sick and tired of the things we produce while in darkness. We have to get to the point where going back and forth between darkness and light is causing us to despise ourselves. When this happens, we are ready to approach God the Father and our Lord Jesus Christ in total truth. The Holy Spirit can now work with us to get us completely covered in the light of Christ.

We have to want to walk in the light of Christ because God is light. We cannot go on pretending and lying about our walk, for God knows the truth. (1 John 1:5–7)

We overcome darkness by walking in the light of Christ and becoming spiritual in our walk on this earth.

Overcome with the Cares of this World: We have to be careful how we interact in this world once we give our life over to Christ. Jesus teaches us that no one can take us out of His arms. However, we also learn in 2 Peter that we can cause ourselves to get entangled again in the cares of this world. If we get entangled again, then things will be worse off for us than it was at the beginning.

> *- 2 Peter 2:20 (NLT)—"And when people escape from the wickedness of the world by knowing our Lord and Savior Jesus Christ and then get tangled up and enslaved by sin again, they are worse off than before."*

Learning to overcome this world is one of the main reasons we are here on earth, so God can count us worthy and holy unto Himself through Christ Jesus. We have to get to a point in Christ and remain there so nothing in this world is worth giving up our salvation in Christ. Even if we suffer in Christ, we can count it all joy because we know God loves and protects us. Through all our pain and suffering, God is always there working to help us see the light. God the Father wants us to live through the precious blood of Christ. We need to get to a place in our lives where nothing can get us to focus on anything else but the will of God. If we learn to overcome through Christ Jesus, our reward will be great. That is a promise from God. (Revelation 21:6–7)

Understanding why we were created, our purpose on earth, and living to fulfill God's will strengthens us to overcome this world and everything in it. This is not our home; if it were so, God would straighten it all out. But Jesus has gone to prepare a place for us so that, when he comes, we will be with him. We must keep our conscience clear and not allow this world and all its destructible riches to confuse us into thinking this is our home. (Hebrews 13:14–16)

What is the Outcome of Overcoming?

If we are to give up all our desires and pleasures to receive what God has planned for us, we should make sure we understand what we are getting. Learning to overcome is not a simple or easy task; it will take a lifetime to achieve. But, as we move forward and mature in Christ, we will start to experience a change in our thinking, actions, and plans. As we experience the goodness of God, the intent is for the Holy Spirit to draw us more and more into His will and presence. As this occurs, our outcomes will change and we will experience God's loving hand in everything we do; nothing is outside of His control. Let's look at some of the transformations we should experience from a changed heart.

Learning to Overcome Creates a Quiet Spirit: One of the greatest areas we should begin to experience a different outcome is in our workplace. As God renews our spirit and we become confident and trust in God the Father and Jesus Christ, our spirit will change. We will become calm, because we understand that nothing can happen to us without God allowing it. Our interaction with our boss no longer produces anger, and we don't get frustrated regarding things at work.

> *- Ecclesiastes 10:4 (NLT)—"If your boss is angry at you, don't quit! A quiet spirit can overcome even great mistakes."*

We believe and understand that everything we do is for God. We work in peace, we look to solve issues in a loving way, and we don't allow ourselves to get out of control. We allow our spirit to be gentle and quiet, knowing that all power and glory is available to us through Christ Jesus.

> *- Ephesians 4:2–3 (NLT)—"Always be humble and gentle. Be patient with each other, making allowance for each other's faults because of your love. Make every effort to keep yourselves united in the Spirit, binding yourselves together with peace."*

Learning to Overcome

We must always remember that, if we are true to God, He will be true to us. Therefore, He will go ahead of us into all areas of our lives, preparing the way for us. Because He is there, we can afford to walk in a gentle and peaceful spirit before everyone. Don't ever take control back from God because you have entered into a difficult situation at work. He knows the situation and how to handle it better than you or I ever could.

Learning to Overcome Gives Us Peace in Jesus Christ: As we begin to change our thinking and bring our bodies into subjection to God's Holy Spirit, we will start seeing the evidence of overcoming. Again, this does not mean we will not continue to experience trials and tribulations. It does mean we will be in a better mindset and spirit to overcome them in a peaceful way. Some of us have some things in us that are so wild, dangerous, and hard to control, that we need God to grant us even more grace and spiritual teachings to help us overcome. The world has us so tangled up that we can't seem to cut some things loose. As we continue to apply sound spiritual teachings and we go deeper into our prayer life, God lets us know that we can have peace in Him. We can put to death that which is in us that we have been fighting most of our lives. And when it comes our way again, the peace of God the Father and our Lord Jesus Christ overshadows us and we can take heart because He has made a way for us to live in peace. (John 16:32–33)

Learning to Overcome Grants Us Christ's Authority: As we give our lives over to Christ, we become his disciples. After the Holy Spirit has taught us how God operates and our sins have been revealed to us so we overcome them, we develop a deep trust in walking in God's ways. We must set aside everything that is in us that is not of God. At some point, God counts us righteous in His sight. We are fitted for service and sent out to bind that which keeps God's people from receiving him. We are given Christ's authority to trample down those things that prevent the Word of God from being effective. We are given the power to overcome the enemy and be fully protected. (Luke 10:19)

Learning to Overcome

Learning to Overcome Frees Us from Death: One of the things I have come to understand is that a lot of people are in total fear of death. No matter how much we go to church, attend services, or spend time in prayer, the fear of death has a deep hold on us. We state that we believe in God, but we don't have enough faith to actually believe that he has taken death away from us. Yes, we still have to die, but we need to be fully persuaded that God the Father and our Lord Jesus Christ has completely defeated death and its sting. So, what is it about death that keeps us so fearful? Do we believe this world is better than the place that Christ has gone to prepare for those who believe? Do we not believe and understand the power of God and that He is in total control of everything? Maybe we have not fully surrendered ourselves so we are not sure that we are one with Christ. Do we still enjoy walking in our sinful nature and that's what makes us fearful? If we still enjoying walking in our sinful nature even though we have been accepted by Christ, then yes, that is a reason to be fearful. But, if we are working to overcome our sinful nature, knowing that God is granting us grace as we learn to overcome, then we don't have to fear death. God is faithful, and He examines our hearts and motives to determine the state of our spirit. And He grants us more and more grace as long as we are working to overcome. When we have worked with the Holy Spirit and put to death all the sin that has been revealed to us, we can stand with Christ in victory. (1 Corinthians 15:54–57)

Learning to Overcome Produces the Good in Us: Some of us have come from some very bad backgrounds, and because of that we have been taught or we have seen some very evil things in this life. Unfortunately, some of these evils things have been engrained in us. Because these things are so bad, we can't bring ourselves to tell anyone about them, but we are haunted in our mind, body, and spirit every day. We try very hard to cover these things up by participating in religious services and activities. We present ourselves as someone who looks the part of a saint, but we know there is something on the inside that is fighting to get out. How can we be born again in Christ and still have such evil desires or thoughts in us? Some may tell you that you are not saved. But, in Romans, we are taught that we are not to be overcome with evil. So, if we are saved, why would Paul feel the need to teach this scripture?

> *- Romans 12:21 (NIV)—"Do not be overcome by evil, but overcome evil with good."*

It is because we have been given a new spirit and that our spirit is connected to God's Spirit. But, our body is still subjected to this world and all the evil and sin therein. Therefore, we have to work to not be controlled by our sinful nature, but allow the Spirit of God to rule over our mind and body. (Romans 8:9–10)

Through the Holy Spirit, we can put to death all the evil that resides inside of our mind and body. We do this by learning to overcome evil by consistently doing good each and every day and living with a clear conscience. So all that we do and think is pleasing to God the Father and our Lord Jesus Christ.

Learning to Overcome Creates a Prayer Life in Us: I am a living testimony that learning to overcome creates a totally different level of prayer life. I believe I was like most people who accepted Jesus Christ; I understood the need to pray. And just like many others, I interjected prayer into my busy schedule when time permitted. When I prayed, it was mostly for things I wanted or people I cared about. I was just looking for God to bless my ideas, agenda, wants, needs, desires, hopes, and dreams. I believed that, if I gave myself to Christ, he would be willing to bless all my desires if I would just spend a little time in church and in prayer. I read the scripture that says "God will supply all our needs through Christ Jesus who loves us." But, I didn't read the scriptures about what God wanted from me in order for Him to supply all my needs through Christ Jesus. As I continued to seek God the Father and Jesus Christ, the Holy Spirit taught me that God requires us to change and be transformed into His likeness. If I want all my needs met, then I need to increase my devotion to God, including my prayer life. We all want to see the miracles of God evident in our lives, much like the disciples in Mark.

Learning to Overcome

- Mark 9:26–29 (NLT)—"Then the spirit screamed and threw the boy into another violent convulsion and left him. The boy appeared to be dead. A murmur ran through the crowd as people said, 'He's dead.' But Jesus took him by the hand and helped him to his feet, and he stood up. Afterward, when Jesus was alone in the house with his disciples, they asked him, 'Why couldn't we cast out that evil spirit?' Jesus replied, 'This kind can be cast out only by prayer.'"

Jesus teaches us that the outcomes we continue to seek come from learning to overcome through prayer. If we want to be a miracle worker for Christ, we need to have a deeper prayer life. God taught me that, if I wanted to truly be a man of God, my prayer life and time needed to be focused on the needs of others and very little time should be spent on praying for my own desires. If we continue to follow Christ and continue to surrender ourselves to his will and plans, then we are protected. Our focus should be on those who are still struggling in unbelief and a sinful lifestyle. Changing who and what we pray for can drastically change the outcome our prayers. Spending more time in prayer and covering everyone you know, friends, and enemies, can have a broader effect than you will ever know. Changing the topic of our prayers from money, businesses, jobs, and material items, into praying for the saving of souls, will change us from a human-nature praying person to a spiritual praying person.

Learning to Overcome Allows God's Light to Shine in Us: It wasn't until God brought me to a point in my walk with Him that I understood accepting Christ did not remove sin from my body nor did it remove the desire to sin. Christ paid the price for my sins, so I am forgiven and accepted by God the Father; but, God's truth was not known to me. In John, we learn of the pureness of God the Father and Christ, which is represented by light, and that we must walk in that same light. We need to allow the blood of Jesus to cleanse us from our sins. We must be open-minded regarding the sins that remain within us as we continue to seek God's truth. If we start walking in the truth of God and confess our sins, then Christ faithfully cleanses us of our sins. If we continue to claim we have no sin even though the truth of God reveals the sin that is in us, then we are calling God a liar regarding that which He has revealed to us. (1 John 1:5–10)

As we continue to allow God's Spirit to examine what is on the inside of us, we need to confess our sins so we can learn to overcome them through Christ's amazing cleansing process so we can walk in his great light. As we fellowship with others, we will be able to share with them how God is light, and through Jesus Christ and God's great love for us, we are able to walk in His truth and light.

Learning to Overcome Teaches Us How to Live: As God the Father and Christ Jesus prepares us for service, it's very important that we allow His teachings to change the way we live. We learn in Titus that we must enjoy sharing with others what God has blessed us with. We should be the kind of people who know how to live our lives wisely and be good stewards over the things God has provided for us. We should be just in the way we deal and interact with other believers and nonbelievers. As we learn to overcome and God the Father and Jesus Christ share more with us, we need to be more devoted to that which we are receiving. It is true that the more we receive; more will be required of us. With the sharing of Godly knowledge, power, and authority, comes the need to have a disciplined lifestyle. If we cannot control how we live as God continues to bless us, we will be held accountable.

> *- Titus 1:8–10 (NLT)—"Rather, he must enjoy having guests in his home, and he must love what is good. He must live wisely and be just. He must live a devout and disciplined life. He must have a strong belief in the trustworthy message he was taught; then he will be able to encourage others with wholesome teaching and show those who oppose it where they are wrong. For there are many rebellious people who engage in useless talk and deceive others."*

Learning to Overcome

We must become a person who loves to do good, and no one has to continue to ask us to do good. We must love pleasing God by doing good all of the time. This requires a strong belief in what God's Spirit has taught us. We not only love doing good, but we also are a strong encouraging force for God through our wholesome teachings. Living a Godly life is not about words, but power.

Learning to Overcome Teaches Us Humility: Humility is normally not an issue when we first give ourselves to Christ because we come to Christ as a broken person and spirit. It's only after we have walked awhile with God and start developing in Christ that it becomes critical that we learn humility. Our human nature likes to enjoy that which is not pleasing to God. When God reveals our gifts and we start seeing the results of our God-given abilities is when pride, arrogance, and a boastful spirit typically spring up inside of us. If we are not grounded in the truth of God, we may react and accept things generated from our Godly gifts as if it is from our own ability. When this happens, we start experiencing issues and we begin to have problems. You may be a person whom God has gifted to speak encouraging words using the Word of God to attract others to Christ. In the past, you walked among God's people, seeking to help anyone and everyone, but now that you are well known, no one can get close to you. What if Jesus had reacted the way we do when success comes our way? Many stories in the Bible would have a different outcome. But, thank God, He sent us a savior who knew how to walk in godly humility, and accomplish the task God the Father sent him to complete. We who understand the gift of humility that comes from God; gladly use it to help ourselves stay in the Spirit of God and to assist others in coming or staying connected to the source of our strength, Jesus Christ.

-Gal 6:1 (NLT)—"Dear brothers and sisters, if another believer is overcome by some sin, you who are godly should gently and humbly help

Learning to Overcome

A true believer in God the Father and Jesus Christ understands that it is not about prosperity; it's about a lost soul crying out to God and a fellow Christian being able to gently and humbly assist another believer in learning to overcome their struggles.

Learning to Overcome Keeps Us Covered in Grace: One wonderful thing God provided for us was and is His grace. God being such a loving Father understood how hard it would be for us to overcome this world. He gave us His word as instructions for us to increase our faith in Him. God the Father sent our Lord and Savior Jesus Christ to personally teach and demonstrate a way for us to please Him through a walk of faith and to redeem us. Because we were born of sin, we needed a way to know what sin was and a way to know how to walk without living in sin; both of these were provided to us by God. What I have been taught about grace from God is that grace is available to those who are seeking God. We may have gone to church and approached the altar confessing our belief because we had problems or were experiencing difficulties that made life hard at that time. We may even go the distance and get baptized, but somewhere in this process, we did not establish a relationship with God, His Son, and His Holy Spirit. Somewhere in this process, we became religious and focused on the rules of God and not on the love of God. Somewhere in this process, we started claiming things of God and not walking in what we believe. Somewhere in this process, we started believing the lies and not bringing our thinking in line with God's Word. Somewhere in this process, we took a wrong turn and got off the path God put us on. Somewhere in this process, we believed that God will keep on accepting us as we continue to carry out our sinful acts and cover us under His grace. But that is not what the Word of God teaches us. As stated in Romans, using any parts of our body as an instrument of evil is not covered under grace. Allowing sin to continue to be our master is not covered under grace. Living as we lived before is not covered under grace. God's grace grants us time to give ourselves completely over to Him so we can overcome. Grace is for those who see themselves dead to evil and alive in Christ. Grace is for those who need time to learn how to use their body as an instrument to bring God glory and time to learn how to fear God.

> - Romans 6:12–14 (NLT) —"Do not let sin control the way you live; do not give in to sinful desires. Do not let any part of your body become an instrument of evil to serve sin. Instead, give yourselves completely to God, for you were dead, but now you have new life. So use your whole body as an instrument to do what is right for the glory of God. Sin is no longer your master, for you no longer live under the requirements of the law. Instead, you live under the freedom of God's grace."

Grace is there for those who are new to Christ so they have time to learn God's ways while they live on milk. Grace is there for those who need time to mature in Christ so they have time to learn God's ways while living on meat. God extends grace to those who are in Christ so they have time to learn of God, learn the love of God, and no one has to continually encourage us to follow Christ.

Learning to Overcome Allows Us to Walk in God's Truth: For me, one of the biggest things I have received from learning to overcome through God's Holy Spirit and Christ Jesus is the ability to walk in God's truth. As with everything God has shown or taught me, this too was a process. As I continued to study God's Word, pray, and seek His face through Christ Jesus and the Holy Spirit, God pointed out to me that I was reasoning everything He was teaching me. I would look at a teaching from the Bible from my perspective and personal experiences. Did I believe in what was been taught or not? I was like most people, who want God's Word to translate into what we want and think is the truth. The more I learned God's Word, the more I tried changing it to mean different things. Then God chastened me about adding, modifying, and changing His Word. He took me to the scriptures (Deuteronomy 12:32, Proverbs 30:6, and Revelation 22:18), where He taught me it is a sin to add, change, or modify the Word of God in our teaching of scripture. I believe that God protects His Word, even when it is translated into different languages. God is working to protect every word He has spoken and will speak, because every word of God is truth and it will come to pass and be fulfilled by His power and authority. Now that I have come to accept God's Word as the unchangeable truth, it has allowed me to become free from reasoning. Now I can pray in God's truth without overlaying His Word with my thoughts or personal beliefs. Now, I can listen to another believer and listen for the Word of God, and allow my spirit to be in agreement with the Word of God from another person of God. Because God is greater than any one person, it takes several godly people working together to complete the work of God.

> *- 1 John 4:4–6 (NIV)—"You, dear children, are from God and have overcome them, because the one who is in you is greater than the one who is in the world. They are from the world and therefore speak from the viewpoint of the world, and the world listens to them. We are from God, and whoever knows God listens to us; but whoever is not from God does not listen to us. This is how we recognize the Spirit of truth and the spirit of falsehood."*

Learning to Overcome Produces the Love of God in Us: As we learn to overcome this world, we draw closer to God the Father and our Lord Jesus Christ. As God teaches us His loving ways, we begin to understand what it means to love God. At first, we think loving God has to do with us loving Him for what He can do for us. As we move into a right relationship with God, we begin to understand that we are not here on this earth to send our many requests up to God so He can bless us. We are here to learn how to love God with all our heart and soul. God teaches us how to accept and follow His commandments, which pleases Him. And as stated in 1 John, we cannot love God if we think His ways are burdensome to us. (1 John 5:3–5)

The only way I know to learn to overcome this world and demonstrate how much we truly love God is by surrendering our whole being to God's purpose. If we try to hold on to this world, we will lose all that God has planned for us. The love of God cannot come from anything we have learned in this world. If we try to apply our perspective of love to how God wants us to love Him and others, we will miss the mark. Again, nothing we have learned in this world can be compared to what God has for us, including what it means to love someone and love God. As we learn to love with godly love, we start producing in God's will and His loving ways. The end result of the perfect Love of God is victory in Christ.

The outcome of us learning to overcome and believing with all our heart in God the Father and our Lord Jesus Christ is becoming a new person. We are no longer that person who first confessed their sins to Christ. We have learned to walk in all situations with a quiet spirit, allowing the Spirit of God to be with us and guide us through all trials and tribulations. We now understand that the peace of Christ is worth more than any sum of money or holding onto our self-righteous thinking. When God starts to use us for His service, we will learn to walk in the authority of Christ. We can walk in freedom and stand in faith, no longer overcome with the fear of death. As we change in Christ, we have the spirit of doing good every day inside of us because we know it pleases God. Our prayer life is greatly expanded, and we spend our prayer time in the spirit covering souls that are suffering and lost. We no longer spend our time going back and forth between darkness and light; we stand firm in the light of God. Our life's endeavor now is to live for God the Father and our Lord Jesus Christ. We no longer live for ourselves; we live for God. Through our deliverance, we are grounded in humility, not seeking to please ourselves, only seeking the will of God. As we continue to mature, we seek God's grace to strengthen us so we do not get discouraged as we learn to overcome and put to death all our sins through Christ Jesus. We walk in confidence that we have a firm understanding of God's Word and truth as He continues to reveal more and more to us. We understand that all things are based on the Love of God, and nothing is based on our abilities or anything in us.

God's Rest

Giving God the Father and Jesus Christ all the Glory: As we start to overcome the things that God has and is showing us that He dislikes in us, we become the person God wants us to be. After we have received a spirit of humility because we understand all things come from God the Father through our Lord Christ Jesus, we can come together with others to give God all the glory. Because you and I have traveled with Christ and learned how to overcome trials and tribulations, we can accept others who are suffering and struggling to overcome. We understand the reason Christ came as a servant is to demonstrate and teach us how to have a servant's heart in pleasing God. (Romans 15:5–9)

We have developed our confidence that God will be true to His promises in helping us to make it through this life. Christ came to reconcile all who love God the Father unto himself so we can experience the freedom to worship and praise God for what He was done for us.

Being Encouraged: As we learn to overcome, our faith should be strengthening in God the Father and our Lord Jesus Christ. As we see more and more evidence that Christ and the Father are actively changing us and our circumstances, our faith should grow. God's acts of kindness, grace, and mercy should encourage us to draw closer for more. As our sins are forgiven, we should be encouraged as we receive healing as when Jesus healed the paralyzed man in Matthew.

> *- Matthew 9:1–2 (NLT)—"Jesus climbed into a boat and went back across the lake to his own town. Some people brought to him a paralyzed man on a mat. Seeing their faith, Jesus said to the paralyzed man, 'Be encouraged, my child! Your sins are forgiven.'"*

Many of us are struggling with all types of issues—sickness, diseases, financial problems, relationship issues, family problems, and even job related issues. When we get to the point where the woman with the issue of bleeding had gotten, where she knew no other option but to demonstrate her faith while others were afraid to approach Christ, he will stop and receive us. Jesus Christ is never too busy to help someone who calls out to him and demonstrates their faith in him. (Matthew 9:20–22)

Because Jesus Christ and God the Father will always remain the same, we can be encouraged that God is faithful and He is a loving God today and tomorrow. God wants us all to be whole. We accomplish this by allowing the Holy Spirit to clean the inside of the cup first and then the outside. Learning to overcome starts on the inside. We must have faith in God and let our faith be manifested in our actions and reactions. Be encouraged because God is more than able.

Able to Help Others: Once we have walked with God and have seen how He helps us overcome, His Holy Spirit equips us for good works by imparting spiritual gifts in us. These gifts are not intended to bring us riches and glory but to be used to serve others and give God all the glory.

> *-1 Peter 4:10–11 (NLT)*—*"God has given each of you a gift from his great variety of spiritual gifts. Use them well to serve one another. Do you have the gift of speaking? Then speak as though God himself were speaking through you. Do you have the gift of helping others? Do it with all the strength and energy that God supplies. Then everything you do will bring glory to God through Jesus Christ. All glory and power to him forever and ever!"*

Learning to overcome is not about getting our needs met, but God meets our needs so we can be free to help others. All of us who have overcome and been delivered can glorify God for what He has done in our lives.

Become Free: One powerful outcome that comes from learning to overcome is becoming free in Christ Jesus and God the Father. Christ sets us free from worrying over material things, worldly desires, our thinking, being selfish, comparing ourselves to others, thinking too much of ourselves and our abilities, and desiring the riches of this world. Think about it: If we did not spend our time and energy on the above-mentioned things, what would we do with our time? We would not spend our time shopping for things we don't need. We would not spend our time dreaming of how great we want to be and how we want others to think of us. We would not spend our time chasing after money as if it's the thing that will provide freedom and happiness. We are no longer slaves to this type of thinking. (Romans 6:15–18)

We must not pick up worldly thinking again once we are set free. We must not get enslaved by continuing to sin. This type of thinking will cause many sins to be re-manifested in our lives. We are set free to serve God the Father and Jesus Christ. We are free to move and do anything that God instructs and guides us to do. We are free to praise God for what He has done and to worship Him for what He is planning to do. We have become slaves to Christ, seeking to please God in every way. Instead of claiming to be righteous, we are set free to walk in the righteousness of God the Father and our Lord Jesus Christ.

Become Pure of Heart: Another end result of learning to overcome is the development of a pure heart. As God examines our heart, mind, spirit, and motives, we need to arrive at a point in Christ where we have overcome all sin or where we are getting close to overcoming all the sin in us that God has shown us that He hates. As this occurs, our heart becomes pure and our thinking and desires are pure because there is nothing sinful in us. Our souls have been cleansed by the Holy Spirit and Christ, and we have overcome this world in the likeness of Christ.

> - *1 Peter 1:22–23 (NKJV)—"Since you have purified your souls in obeying the truth through the Spirit in sincere love of the brethren, love one another fervently with a pure heart, having been born again, not of corruptible seed but incorruptible, through the word of God which lives and abides forever."*

We will know we are operating with a pure heart because our desires, wants, and needs have nothing to do with what we want. We care about God's desires and for the happiness of others. God the Father and Christ will see our obedience and reward us by blessing our actions. We of pure hearts will see our blessings as a confirmation that we are doing the work God called us to do so we will take the blessings and do more for God and others. A pure heart is pure because self is not involved.

Receiving God's Rest: By now we have overcome our sinful nature and we have control over our human nature because we live in Christ Jesus. We seek and allow the Holy Spirit to renew us each day as we carry out the work that God has assigned us. We are granted God's rest so our hearts and soul are at rest, free from worry and defeat. We have the victory of Christ in us, and we stand fully armored with the armor of salvation. Nothing in this world can turn us from focusing on God's plan and purpose. We know what it means to overcome because we have been tested and have passed every test. We know the voice of God, and we freely share God's teachings and blessings with others. We who believe enter into God's rest.

> *- Hebrews 4:1–3 (NLT)—"God's promise of entering his rest still stands, so we ought to tremble with fear that some of you might fail to experience it. For this good news—that God has prepared this rest—has been announced to us just as it was to them. But it did them no good because they didn't share the faith of those who listened to God. For only we who believe can enter his rest."*

Receiving a Reward: Learning to overcome and placing our trust and hope in God the Father and Jesus Christ means we will be rewarded for our good deeds. There are two ways we can receive our reward. We could request God to bless us with our reward while here on earth, or we could follow the instructions of Christ Jesus and store up our reward in heaven where it does not fade away. We must understand that we will only be rewarded once for a deed well-done, so be careful where you seek your reward. We learn in Revelation that we must wash our robes by being purified in Christ. We will be permitted to enter into the gates of the Kingdom of God, and there we will be given the fruit of life to eat. No more death, no more sickness, no more diseases.

> *- Rev 22:12–15 (NLT)—"Look, I am coming soon, bringing my reward with me to repay all people according to their deeds. I am the Alpha and the Omega, the First and the Last, the Beginning and the End. Blessed are those who wash their robes. They will be permitted to enter through the gates of the city and eat the fruit from the tree of life. Outside the city are the dogs—the sorcerers, the sexually immoral, the murderers, the idol worshipers, and all who love to live a lie."*

It is done. Our Lord Jesus Christ has shown us the way, and we have listened to every word of God and placed it in our hearts. We have learned to overcome by listening to the voice of God and learning to fear Him. We seek God's ways and His face, discarding our own thinking and desires. Great is the reward that Christ brings when he comes. Great is the Kingdom of God and His loving ways, and great is the Christ of God. Well done, good and faithful servant.

A Prayer for Those Who Overcome

Father, in the name of our Lord Jesus Christ, we thank you for accepting us.

When we confessed our sins, you were faithful in forgiving us.

When we transgressed as we learned to overcome, you granted us grace.

As we moved from drinking milk to eating meat, you extended your grace.

When trials and tribulations came upon us, you were there.

When addictions come upon us or a loved one, you were there.

When we experienced grief and sorrow, you were there.

When fear gripped us, you were there.

When we were being haunted in our dreams, you gave us relief.

When we struggled with overcoming our anger, you gave us peace.

When we had a hard time overcoming our unbelief, you continued to love us.

When life kept knocking us down; you picked us up.

When worldly desires kept pressing upon us, you gave us a way out.

When Satan cast darkness over us, you provided your great light.

Thank you for covering us with you grace as we learn to overcome.

Thank you for teaching us how to be good by being our example.

Thank you for your Holy Spirit so we can be taught your truth.

Thank you for teaching us the Love of God because we didn't know love.

Thank you for accepting me as I was and changing me to who I am.

Learning to Overcome Life

The purpose of this chart is to provide a visual understanding of the content in this chapter. The reader can use this chart to help evaluate where they are in terms of learning to overcome any false or ungodly beliefs and practices that go against the will of God the Father and our Lord Jesus Christ. Many of us get our beliefs and understanding from being raised in a particular church or a religion. Then, there are those who bring their worldly understanding with them into the church, along with their worldly belief system. But, we have not developed our beliefs and understandings purely on the Word of God; therefore, we struggle with life because we are still holding on to and struggling with issues that should have been dead in us a long time ago.

For us to live within the presence of God as we desire in our hearts, we must be willing to learn through the Word of God how to overcome and become victorious even while we walk on the Earth. Nothing is impossible for God; things only seem impossible in our minds.

Learning to Overcome

An Overcomers Lifestyle

Changing from Darkness to the Light of Christ

You cannot be found in the Middle

Our Will and Purpose
Produces a Sinful Nature
Old Self

God's Will and Purpose
Produces a Righteous Person
New Creation

Our Self-Righteousness

God's Holiness

The Presence of God

Learning to Overcome

The Great Chasm Between God and Man Worlds - Luke 14:26

- The Presence of God is worth more than our desire to be rich
- The Presence of God is worth more than the materialistic things we desire
- The Presence of God is worth more than the pleasures we enjoy
- The Presence of God is worth more than us being right
- The Presence of God is worth more than us being in control or in charge
- The Presence of God is worth more than finding a husband or a wife

- The Presence of God is worth more, than the career or position we hold
- The Presence of God is worth more, than the education we have obtained
- The Presence of God is worth more, than our family members
- The Presence of God is worth more than the power we thirst to possess
- The Presence of God is worth more, than any selfish desire or act
- The Presence of God is worth more, than any of our relationships

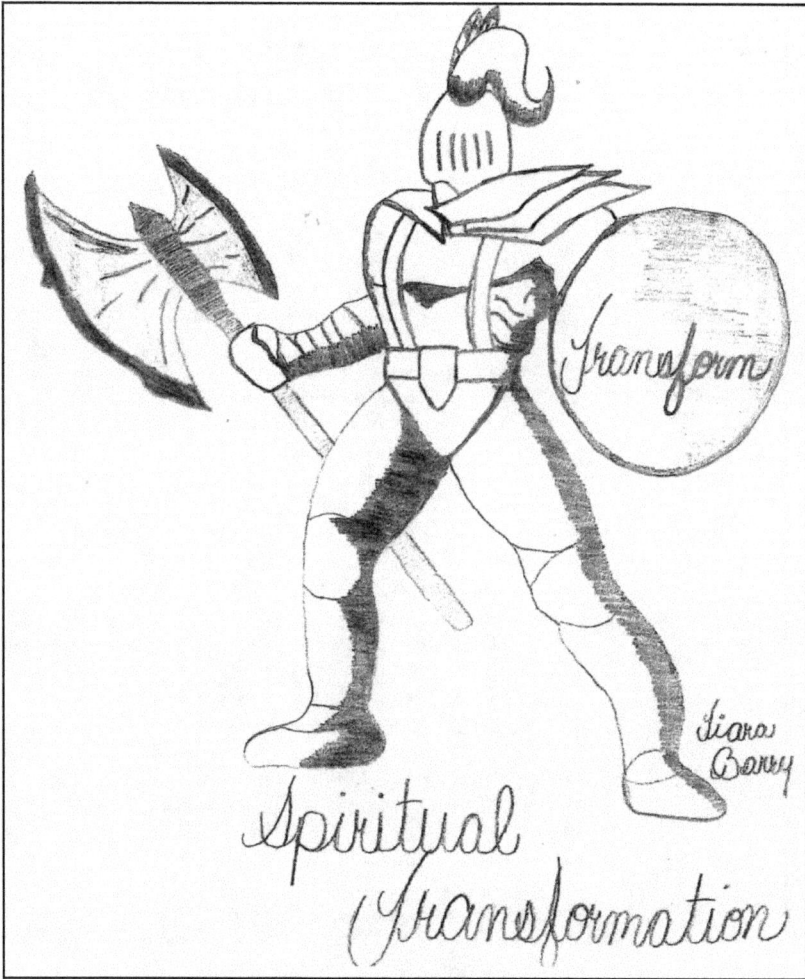

Spiritual Transformation

Chapter 4

A STATE OF BEING

by Donna Maria Barry

When I looked I could not see it
It wasn't there
There wasn't anything
Emptiness was in its' place

Sounds invaded its' privacy
Though silence was still present
Movements went unnoticed
Stillness was a welcomed friend

Thoughts were suspended
Thinking brought about tears
Feelings were not understood
Reasoning seemed very cloudy

Inquiries sought information
Words spoken were senseless
Communication came and went
Relationships were disconnected

Safety meant everything
Security was not negotiable
Depression was a state of being
GOD had to come to the rescue

Once touched by GOD it began to renew
The beauty of restoration took control
Noticeable changes became the obvious
Clearly transformation was in progress

The process has been timely
The results are apparent. It is there
It stands proudly with its head held high
And clinches a redefined purpose in its hand

Its spoken of as a Conqueror
Proclamations of victory ring out
When last I saw it, it was in an arena
Receiving a standing ovation

Spiritual Transformation

From the beginning, God was and is seeking to have a group of people who are dedicated to his purpose and will. God wants a group of people He can bless and, in return, receive their praise and worship. God wants this group of people to choose Him as their God and accept His plan for their lives. But, we have decided to live in sin rather than to be blessed by God's perfect plan and purpose for us. He then decided to send His Son to prove to us how much He truly loves us. Through and by Christ Jesus, we have a divine way to develop a relationship with God the Father. Through this new way, God is preparing a people for himself, and it requires us to go through a transformation, so we can become spiritual, because God is a Spirit. God's will is for those who are called by His name to accept and learn from our Lord God and Savior Christ Jesus. The outcome of completing the transformation is for us to pass through Christ's Final Judgment with confidence, to be accepted into God's Kingdom, to receive a reward for our good deeds, and to receive eternal life.

> *- Revelation 21:5–7 (NLT)—"And the one sitting on the throne said, 'Look, I am making everything new!' And then he said to me, 'Write this down, for what I tell you is trustworthy and true.' And he also said, 'It is finished! I am the Alpha and the Omega—the Beginning and the End. To all who are thirsty I will give freely from the springs of the water of life. All who are victorious will inherit all these blessings, and I will be their God, and they will be my children.'"*

Let's discuss the transformation! We will cover the following four areas of transformation.

- The beginning of spiritual transformation
- The transformation process (the preparation)
- Growing through spiritual transformation
- The outcome of spiritual transformation

Spiritual Transformation

It all begins by believing in God the Father and Christ Jesus: It is impossible to be transformed without believing and accepting Christ Jesus.

To have eternal life and for our souls to never die, we must accept Jesus Christ. (John 11:25–26)

Believing in Jesus Christ means we will never be alone and he will never abandon us.

> *- John 14:18–21 (NLT)—"No, I will not abandon you as orphans— I will come to you. Soon the world will no longer see me, but you will see me. Since I live, you also will live. When I am raised to life again, you will know that I am in my Father, and you are in me, and I am in you. Those who accept my commandments and obey them are the ones who love me. And because they love me, my Father will love them. And I will love them and reveal myself to each of them."*

Accepting Jesus the Christ as your Lord and Savior: There is no other way to salvation and eternal life except through Christ Jesus. He is the true shepherd, those who believe; belong to the good shepherd, and not to the hired hand.

> *- John 10:7–16 (NLT)—"I tell you the truth, I am the gate for the sheep. All who came before me were thieves and robbers. But the true sheep did not listen to them. Yes, I am the gate. Those who come in through me will be saved. They will come and go freely and will find good pastures. The thief's purpose is to steal and kill and destroy. My purpose is to give them a rich and satisfying life. I am the good shepherd. The good shepherd sacrifices his life for the sheep. A hired hand will run when he sees a wolf coming. He will abandon the sheep because they don't belong to him and he isn't their shepherd. And so the wolf attacks them and scatters the flock. The hired hand runs away because he's working only for the money and doesn't really care about the sheep. I am the good shepherd; I know my own sheep, and they know me, just as my Father knows me and I know the Father. So I sacrifice my life for the sheep. I have other sheep, too, that are not in this sheepfold. I must bring them also. They will listen to my voice, and there will be one flock with one shepherd."*

Confession and Repentance of Sin and the Fulfillment of Baptism is a Requirement: Being accepted requires us to confess and repent; being baptized without confessing and repenting will prevent us from receiving the Holy Spirit.

We are required to confess that Jesus Christ is our Lord.

- Matthew 10:32–33 (NKJV)—"Therefore whoever confesses Me before men, him I will also confess before My Father who is in heaven. But whoever denies Me before men, him I will also deny before My Father who is in heaven."

We need to confess our sins, and be properly baptized.

- Mark 1:4–5 (NKJV)—"John came baptizing in the wilderness and preaching a baptism of repentance for the remission of sins. Then all the land of Judea, and those from Jerusalem, went out to him and were all baptized by him in the Jordan River, confessing their sins."

The presence of the Holy Spirit should be a sign to those who are baptized.

- Mark 16:16–18 (KJV)—"He that believeth and is baptized shall be saved; but he that believeth not shall be damned. And these signs shall follow them that believe; In my name shall they cast out devils; they shall speak with new tongues; They shall take up serpents; and if they drink any deadly thing, it shall not hurt them; they shall lay hands on the sick, and they shall recover."

Repenting, turning to God, and being baptized in the name of Jesus Christ ensures that we will receive the Holy Spirit.

- Acts 2:38–39 (NLT)—"Peter replied, 'Each of you must repent of your sins, turn to God, and be baptized in the name of Jesus Christ to show that you have received forgiveness for your sins. Then you will receive the gift of the Holy Spirit. This promise is to you, and to your children, and even to the Gentiles—all who have been called by the Lord our God.'"

Confessing and believing in our hearts that Jesus Christ is the Son of God allows us to be saved.

- Romans 10:9–10 (NLT)—"If you confess with your mouth that Jesus is Lord and believe in your heart that God raised him from the dead, you will be saved. For it is by believing in your heart that you are made right with God, and it is by confessing with your mouth that you are saved."

Confessing our sins allows us to be forgiven; we cannot walk around claiming we are without sin.

- John 1:8–10 (NLT)—"If we claim we have no sin, we are only fooling ourselves and not living in the truth. But if we confess our sins to him, he is faithful and just to forgive us our sins and to cleanse us from all wickedness. If we claim we have not sinned, we are calling God a liar and showing that his word has no place in our hearts."

A key part of the transformation process was completed by Christ Jesus without any assistance from those who needed a way for their sins to be forgiven. Christ Jesus, in loving obedience to God the Father, stepped up and paid the price so you and I can experience spiritual transformation.

We were bought at a high price; we should no longer live for ourselves.

- 1 Corinthians 6:19–20 (NLT)—"Don't you realize that your body is the temple of the Holy Spirit, who lives in you and was given to you by God? You do not belong to yourself, for God bought you with a high price. So you must honor God with your body."

God has fulfilled His promise and wiped away all our sins.

- Acts 3:18-20 (NLT)—"But God was fulfilling what all the prophets had foretold about the Messiah—that he must suffer these things. Now repent of your sins and turn to God, so that your sins may be wiped away."

We must be willing to surrender and give up our lives to follow Jesus.

- Luke 9:23–25 (NLT)—"Then he said to the crowd, 'If any of you wants to be my follower, you must turn from your selfish ways, take up your cross daily, and follow me. If you try to hang on to

your life, you will lose it. But if you give up your life for my sake, you will save it. And what do you benefit if you gain the whole world but are yourself lost or destroyed."

We must become dead to our sinful ways and our self; we cannot mix the old with the new.

- Romans 6:10–14 (NLT)—"When he died, he died once to break the power of sin. But now that he lives, he lives for the glory of God. So you also should consider yourselves to be dead to the power of sin and alive to God through Christ Jesus. Do not let sin control the way you live; do not give in to sinful desires. Do not let any part of your body become an instrument of evil to serve sin. Instead, give yourselves completely to God, for you were dead, but now you have new life."

- Mark 2:22 (NLT)—"And no one puts new wine into old wineskins. For the wine would burst the wineskins, and the wine and the skins would both be lost. New wine calls for new wineskins."

There is no way we can remain saved in our current state; we must be born again to enter into the Kingdom of God.

- John 3:3 (NLT)—"Jesus replied, 'I tell you the truth, unless you are born again, you cannot see the Kingdom of God."

A new heart and spirit is needed within us to allow God's transformation process to lead us into obedience.

- Ezekiel 36:26–27 (NLT)—"And I will give you a new heart, and I will put a new spirit in you. I will take out your stony, stubborn heart and give you a tender, responsive heart. And I will put my Spirit in you so that you will follow my decrees and be careful to obey my regulations."

God provided a way through Christ for us to have a wonderful new relationship with Him and Christ Jesus.

- Romans 5:8–11 (NLT)—"But God showed his great love for us by sending Christ to die for us while we were still sinners. And since we have been made right in God's sight by the blood of Christ, he will certainly save us from God's condemnation. For since our friendship with God was restored by the death of

his Son while we were still his enemies, we will certainly be saved through the life of his Son. So now we can rejoice in our wonderful new relationship with God because our Lord Jesus Christ has made us friends of God."

We must not be so quick to rush through the beginning of our salvation because we will have to start over if we don't accept and receive Christ Jesus correctly. We cannot enter into the transformation process without the Holy Spirit. Going forward without confessing, repenting, and receiving the Holy Spirit, means you will be claiming to be a child of God with very little results from your words. The Kingdom of God is about power and not words. We have to begin by drinking spiritual milk.

- 1 Peter 2:2 (NLT)—"Like newborn babies, you must crave pure spiritual milk so that you will grow into a full experience of salvation."

The Transformation Process (The Preparation)

Now that we know what it takes to become a believer and how to receive the Holy Spirit, we can put our focus on Christ Jesus as our good shepherd. He will then come and teach us everything we need to know, making us fit to learn from him and put to death everything in us that goes against God's will. In John, we learn that the Holy Spirit will teach us the truth about God the Father and our Lord Jesus Christ. (1 John 2:26)

As we grow in fellowship with Christ, he starts preparing us for the purpose for which we were created. It's important to understand that the time of preparation is not defined by us; neither do we determine when it's over. The goal of the preparation process is for us to come to a complete understanding about God the Father and our Lord Jesus Christ. We must be prepared for service and guided so we can achieve what God planned from the beginning of time. As we read in 2nd Timothy, We need to study the Word of God, so we can understand what is wrong in our lives.

- 2 Timothy 3:16–17 (NLT), "All Scripture is inspired by God and is useful to teach us what is true and to make us realize what is wrong in our lives. It corrects us when we are wrong and teaches us to do what is right. God uses it to prepare and equip his people to do every good work." *Since God uses His Word as a preparation tool, let's get a complete picture of what God wants us to learn.*

Learning God's Word: It's important to learn God's word because it contains God's truth, including His ways. His word allows the Holy Spirit to teach us about God. When God has something to teach us, His Holy Spirit uses the Word of God as a reference point so we can obtain true teaching and we will be able to distinguish His voice from Satan's or our own.

Accepting God's Word

- James 1:21–23 (NLT)—"So get rid of all the filth and evil in your lives, and humbly accept the word God has planted in your hearts, for it has the power to save your souls. But don't just listen to God's word. You must do what it says. Otherwise, you are only fooling yourselves. For if you listen to the word and don't obey, it is like glancing at your face in a mirror."

Standing firm on God's Word

- Luke 21:14–19 (NLT)—"So don't worry in advance about how to answer the charges against you, for I will give you the right words and such wisdom that none of your opponents will be able to reply or refute you! Even those closest to you—your parents, brothers, relatives, and friends—will betray you. They will even kill some of you. And everyone will hate you because you are my followers. But not a hair of your head will perish! By standing firm, you will win your souls."

Warnings about adding or changing God's Word

- Deuteronomy 12:32 (NKJV)—"Whatever I command you, be careful to observe it; you shall not add to it nor take away from it."

-Proverbs 30:6 (NKJV)—"Do not add to His words, lest He rebuke you, and you be found a liar."

- Revelation 22:18–19 (NKJV)—*"For I testify to everyone who hears the words of the prophecy of this book: If anyone adds to these things, God will add to him the plagues that are written in this book; and if anyone takes away from the words of the book of this prophecy, God shall take away his part from the Book of Life, from the holy city, and from the things which are written in this book."*

Learning to love: Given that we are born of sin, how is it we perceive that we know how to love or be loved? The love of God is nothing like the love we were taught or experienced growing up in this world. It is not based on our emotions, what we see, what we feel, what we want, or what we think. The love of God is pure; it is not based on conditions. It does not reject, it comforts. It encourages and provides peace and joy. It's based on truth, and it cares for the lost. It cares for the wronged, and it cares for the hopeless. It covers those in need, and it does not divide. It bonds those who love God, and spreads to those who believe in Christ Jesus. Therefore, we are made complete in Christ, to the glory of God the Father. Without applying the love of God to our transformation process, we cannot grow and achieve true transformation.

Experience the love of God the Father and Christ Jesus so we can be made complete.

- Ephesians 3:17–19 (NLT)—*"Then Christ will make his home in your hearts as you trust in him. Your roots will grow down into God's love and keep you strong. And may you have the power to understand, as all God's people should, how wide, how long, how high, and how deep his love is. May you experience the love of Christ, though it is too great to understand fully. Then you will be made complete with all the fullness of life and power that comes from God."*

Once we learn God's love and it is complete in us, we can then demonstrate the love of God to others.

- 1 John 2:3–6 (NLT)—*"And we can be sure that we know him if we obey his commandments. If someone claims, 'I know God,' but doesn't obey God's commandments, that person is a liar and is*

not living in the truth. But those who obey God's word truly show how completely they love him. That is how we know we are living in him. Those who say they live in God should live their lives as Jesus did."

The outcome of Godly love is having love for our brothers and sisters; if we fail to demonstrate Godly love, then God is not in us.

- 1 John 4:16–21 (NIV)—"Whoever lives in love lives in God, and God in him. In this way, love is made complete among us so that we will have confidence on the day of judgment, because in this world we are like him. There is no fear in love. But perfect love drives out fear, because fear has to do with punishment. The one who fears is not made perfect in love. We love because he first loved us. If anyone says, 'I love God,' yet hates his brother, he is a liar. For whoever does not love his brother, whom he has seen, cannot love God, whom he has not seen. And he has given us this command: Whoever loves God must also love his brother."

As they say, love is the key. Without love, there will be no forgiveness because we haven't truly forgiven. Without love, there will be no grace because we haven't truly repented. Without love, there is no mercy because we haven't shown mercy to others. Without love, there is no prosperity because we don't love others enough to share. Without love, there is no peace because we continue to hate, argue, and fight with others. Without love, there is no joy because we don't understand how to be happy. Without love, there is no God because God is love.

Learning God's Ways: From the beginning, God has taken the time to impart His loving ways to His chosen people. He has a few requirements that we must adhere to for us to experience the loving ways of God. We must walk in truth, accept His Son, and maintain a clear conscience so God can declare us righteous.

We must always walk in God's truth, no matter what.

> *- 2 Timothy 2:19 (NLT)—"But God's truth stands firm like a foundation stone with this inscription: 'The Lord knows those who are his,' and 'All who belong to the Lord must turn away from evil.'"*

Many times, God allows us to see that which He had planned; it takes obedience to see things through God's Eyes.

> *- Acts 26:15–18 (NLT)—"'Who are you, lord?' I asked. And the Lord replied, 'I am Jesus, the one you are persecuting. Now get to your feet! For I have appeared to you to appoint you as my servant and witness. You are to tell the world what you have seen and what I will show you in the future. And I will rescue you from both your own people and the Gentiles. Yes, I am sending you to the Gentiles to open their eyes, so they may turn from darkness to light and from the power of Satan to God.'"*

Just claiming to believe in Jesus is not enough, if we truly believe in him, we would do what he says.

> *- John 14:21 (NLT)—"Those who accept my commandments and obey them are the ones who love me. And because they love me, my Father will love them. And I will love them and reveal myself to each of them."*

To live our life based on God's ways requires us to maintain and live with a clear consequence.

> *- 1 Peter 3:15–16 (NLT)—"Instead, you must worship Christ as Lord of your life. And if someone asks about your Christian hope, always be ready to explain it. But do this in a gentle and respectful way. Keep your conscience clear. Then if people speak against you, they will be ashamed when they see what a good life you live because you belong to Christ."*

Learning to Master Sin: One of the main reasons we are here on earth is to develop our ability to master sin. The main purpose for the law of Moses was to define sin for us so we can understand what it means to sin and what actions cause God to turn from us. In Revelation, Christ Jesus rewards those who have overcome, as we achieve maturity in Christ and master self-control.

The way we live is evidence that we have repented for our sins; it's not in what we say.

- Matthew 3:8–9 (NLT)—"Prove by the way you live that you have repented of your sins and turned to God. Don't just say to each other, 'We're safe, for we are descendants of Abraham.' That means nothing, for I tell you, God can create children of Abraham from these very stones."

We have to be honest with ourselves and not be stubborn and refuse to recognize our sin.

- Romans 2:5–8 (NLT)—"But because you are stubborn and refuse to turn from your sin, you are storing up terrible punishment for yourself. For a day of anger is coming, when God's righteous judgment will be revealed. He will judge everyone according to what they have done. He will give eternal life to those who keep on doing good, seeking after the glory and honor and immortality that God offers. But he will pour out his anger and wrath on those who live for themselves, who refuse to obey the truth and instead live lives of wickedness."

We must understand that temptation will come upon everyone, but we have to keep watch so we are not overtaken with temptation.

- Matthew 26:41 (NLT)—"Keep watch and pray, so that you will not give in to temptation. For the spirit is willing, but the body is weak!"

We must be willing to help one another overcome sin and not be prideful by not helping others and to keep our own selves free from sin.

- Galatians 6:1–3 (NLT)—"Dear brothers and sisters, if another believer is overcome by some sin, you who are godly should gently and humbly help that person back onto the right path. And be careful not to fall into the same temptation yourself. Share each other's burdens, and in this way obey the law of Christ. If you think you are too important to help someone, you are only fooling yourself. You are not that important."

Spiritual Transformation

Each and every day we must count ourselves dead to sin; we must put to death every sinful act in the body.

> *- Romans 6:7–13 (NLT)—"For when we died with Christ we were set free from the power of sin. And since we died with Christ, we know we will also live with him. We are sure of this because Christ was raised from the dead, and he will never die again. Death no longer has any power over him. When he died, he died once to break the power of sin. But now that he lives, he lives for the glory of God. So you also should consider yourselves to be dead to the power of sin and alive to God through Christ Jesus. Do not let sin control the way you live; do not give in to sinful desires. Do not let any part of your body become an instrument of evil to serve sin. Instead, give yourselves completely to God, for you were dead, but now you have new life."*

Mastering self-control allows us to reach the holy place God has called us into.

> *- 1 Peter 1:13-16 (NLT)—"So think clearly and exercise self-control. Look forward to the gracious salvation that will come to you when Jesus Christ is revealed to the world. So you must live as God's obedient children. Don't slip back into your old ways of living to satisfy your own desires. You didn't know any better then. But now you must be holy in everything you do, just as God who chose you is holy. For the Scriptures say, 'You must be holy because I am holy.'*

We must be transformed from carrying out sin by submitting our mind, body, thinking, and spirit to God's spirit. Satan is hard at work getting us to believe lies about God. From the beginning, Satan reasoned with man to not believe the very words of God. Even today, we compromise the Word of God for our own pleasures, thinking grace will allow us to be accepted as we continue to sin. But God the Father and our Lord Christ Jesus continues to be hard at work teaching us to deny our own thinking and get into right thinking with God, so we can overcome sin and be declared victorious at the end of the race.

Spiritual Transformation

Learning to Live by Faith: As we continue allowing the Holy Spirit to transform us into the image of Christ, we must start living by faith. Again, this is not a matter of words; faith does not come just by us stating that we have faith. But it is a matter of actually walking by faith in everything we do, say, and think. We need to get to the point where we are allowing God to be in total control of our lives. We count ourselves of no great value without Christ instructing us and guiding us in all our thinking, decisions, actions, and purpose. We do it all to give God the Father all the glory for transforming us in our daily walk.

We must learn to stand in the faith that we speak about with our words.

> *- 1 Corinthians 10:11–13 (NIV)—"These things happened to them as examples and were written down as warnings for us, on whom the fulfillment of the ages has come. So, if you think you are standing firm, be careful that you don't fall! No temptation has seized you except what is common to man. And God is faithful; he will not let you be tempted beyond what you can bear. But when you are tempted, he will also provide a way out so that you can stand up under it."*

As we learn to live by faith, God will protect us.

> *- Psalms 121:1–8 (NIV)—"I lift up my eyes to the hills—where does my help come from? My help comes from the Lord, the Maker of heaven and earth. He will not let your foot slip—he who watches over you will not slumber; indeed, he who watches over Israel will neither slumber nor sleep. The Lord watches over you—the Lord is your shade at your right hand; the sun will not harm you by day, nor the moon by night. The Lord will keep you from all harm—he will watch over your life; the Lord will watch over your coming and going both now and forevermore."*

We must understand that we cannot live in the middle of the road; this is not a place for those who walk in faith.

> *- Revelation 3:14–17 (NIV)—These are the words of the Amen, the faithful and true witness, the ruler of God's creation. I know your deeds, that you are neither cold nor hot. I wish you were*

either one or the other! So, because you are lukewarm—neither hot nor cold—I am about to spit you out of my mouth. You say, 'I am rich; I have acquired wealth and do not need a thing.' But you do not realize that you are wretched, pitiful, poor, blind and naked."

We must be able to demonstrate our faith to God and others, even in the time of trouble.

- Luke 8:24–25 (NIV)—"The disciples went and woke him, saying, 'Master, Master, we're going to drown!' He got up and rebuked the wind and the raging waters; the storm subsided, and all was calm. 'Where is your faith?' he asked his disciples."

Walking by faith is who we are; it's not something we tell people we do. As God looks down upon us, He is looking for a group of people who live by faith. They are not quick to abandon the Word of God for the foolishness of this world. He is looking for a group of people who totally place their trust in the Lord. He is looking for a group of people who treasure being in His presence more than having the riches of this world. God is looking for you and I to live and have faith in His Word, power, and promises, and in our Lord Christ Jesus.

Learning Contentment: Becoming content is very crucial to the transformation process and to its completion. In the Bible, we learn that God grants prosperity to those who follow His will. We also learn that we are required to be content in our wages, in our current condition, and to refrain from being in love with money. (1 Timothy 6:1)

I believe God's ways allow us to produce prosperity and, at the same time, allow overflow into the lives of others by our willingness to become content. The love of money keeps us from learning how to become content with God's blessings.

- Hebrews 13:5 (NIV)—"Keep your lives free from the love of money and be content with what you have, because God has said, 'Never will I leave you; never will I forsake you.'"

We have to be content so we can be satisfied with what we have and where God has us.

> - *Ecclesiastes 1:8 (NLT)—"Everything is wearisome beyond description. No matter how much we see, we are never satisfied. No matter how much we hear, we are not content."*

We cannot allow our desire to become rich, overtake us to the point that we are willing to extort or deal falsely.

> - *Luke 3:14 (NLT)—"'What should we do?' asked some soldiers. John replied, 'Don't extort money or make false accusations. And be content with your pay.'"*

To live a life that is satisfied and content, we have to give careful thought to our ways so God can see the contentment in our hearts.

> - *Haggai 1:5–6—"Now this is what the Lord Almighty says: 'Give careful thought to your ways. You have planted much, but have harvested little. You eat, but never have enough. You drink, but never have your fill. You put on clothes, but are not warm. You earn wages, only to put them in a purse with holes in it.'"*

Paul taught what it means to live content; both, when he was fully supplied or when he had to go without (Philippians 4:11). His message to us is that nothing on this earth is worth forfeiting the opportunity and experience of walking with God. Paul then described the things of this world as garbage; all to be thrown away. One thing is true; no matter how much you and I work and spend money on things in this world, these items will all fade away. As we are transformed into Christ's likeness, we will come to understand how meaningless it is to work so hard for things that are only enjoyable for a short period. We must focus on those things that will never fade away. God wants to know if we are still holding onto selfish desires on the inside. Can we really put others before ourselves? Is God the real treasure of our heart, mind, and soul? God searches these things to discover what's truly on the inside of us. We must learn to be content, for God is in control of all things.

Learning to Trust in God: I cannot share enough, the importance of learning to trust in God the Father and our Lord Christ Jesus. God knows just how much we trust in Him when financial troubles, marriage issues, sexual desires, and job-related issues, come our way and we are found still standing firm on His promises. Not letting life disconnect us from the love of God and His spiritual direction will keep us in God's presence. I know I have mentioned this many times, but trusting in God is not achieved by our words or by us claiming to be a follower and yet not doing what the Word of God commands us to do. Our trust will be tested, and we have to demonstrate that we really believe in the words we speak.

Trust begins with obedience in that which God has shared with you.

> *- Isaiah 26:8–9 (NLT)—"Lord, we show our trust in you by obeying your laws; our heart's desire is to glorify your name. All night long I search for you; in the morning I earnestly seek for God."*

We must learn to hear the voice of God and deny our own voice so we can place our trust in the right source and live holy.

> *- John 5:25 (NLT)—"And I assure you that the time is coming, indeed it's here now, when the dead will hear my voice—the voice of the Son of God. And those who listen will live."*

Learning to trust in God starts with learning to listen and understand His teachings.

> *- Matthew 13:12 (NLT)—"To those who listen to my teaching, more understanding will be given, and they will have an abundance of knowledge. But for those who are not listening, even what little understanding they have will be taken away from them."*

Because God loves us, He will discipline those whom He loves. We can trust that God's discipline is always for our good.

> *- Hebrews 12:7–11 (NLT)—"As you endure this divine discipline, remember that God is treating you as his own children. Who ever heard of a child who is never disciplined by its father? If God doesn't discipline you as he does all of his children, it means that*

you are illegitimate and are not really his children at all. Since we respected our earthly fathers who disciplined us, shouldn't we submit even more to the discipline of the Father of our spirits, and live forever? For our earthly fathers disciplined us for a few years, doing the best they knew how. But God's discipline is always good for us, so that we might share in his holiness. No discipline is enjoyable while it is happening—it's painful! But afterward there will be a peaceful harvest of right living for those who are trained in this way."

Trust goes both ways; we must learn to trust in God and allow God to see us devoting ourselves to doing His will.

- Titus 3:8 (NLT)—"This is a trustworthy saying, and I want you to insist on these teachings so that all who trust in God will devote themselves to doing good. These teachings are good and beneficial for everyone."

To move forward in the transformation process, requires that a mutual trust be established between you and Christ Jesus. Without this trust, there will be no spiritual growth. Many of us spend a lot of time in the preparation stage of transformation because of a trust issue. God is not here for us to pray that He will do our will. We are here to trust that His will is better than anything we could ever imagine for ourselves. Learning to trust in God is a must for all believers. Again, it's not about what we think, but it is about what God has planned for us. How great is His love for us, if we just learn to trust in Hm.

Learning to Let Go: Learning to let go of things in this world is one of the most challenging tasks we are required to perform, to achieve salvation. God makes it clear that we cannot serve two masters; we have to either accept this world or accept God's plan for our lives. It's impossible to please God and be focused on the things in the world. There are so many people who give their lives to Christ for the hope of being blessed in order to obtain worldly riches. We read in the Bible that this is not a desire for a true believer.

- James 5:1–3 (NLT)—"Look here, you rich people: Weep and groan with anguish because of all the terrible troubles ahead of you. Your wealth is rotting away, and your fine clothes are moth-eaten rags. Your gold and silver have become worthless. The very wealth you were counting on will eat away your flesh like fire. This treasure you have accumulated will stand as evidence against you on the day of judgment."

It's important that a true believer worship God in the spirit of truth, and not based on their desires for the things in this world. We should store up our real reward in heaven and not work to store up riches in a world that is fading away. Let's learn to put our desires, hopes, and dreams on the things above and give God all the glory.

We have to let go of our worldly desires and focus on the desires that please God.

- Philippians 2:12–15 (NLT)—"Work hard to show the results of your salvation, obeying God with deep reverence and fear. For God is working in you, giving you the desire and the power to do what pleases him. Do everything without complaining and arguing, so that no one can criticize you. Live clean, innocent lives as children of God, shining like bright lights in a world full of crooked and perverse people."

We have to let go of our thinking and reasoning and not allow human thinking to lead us away from Christ.

- Colossians 2:8–10 (NLT)—"Don't let anyone capture you with empty philosophies and high-sounding nonsense that come from human thinking and from the spiritual powers of this world, rather than from Christ. For in Christ lives all the fullness of God in a human body. So you also are complete through your union with Christ, who is the head over every ruler and authority."

We have to learn to let go of those who falsely lead us into deceptive lifestyles, luring those who have escaped into becoming tangled up and enslaved all over again.

Spiritual Transformation

- 2 Peter 2:18–21 (NLT)—"They brag about themselves with empty, foolish boasting. With an appeal to twisted sexual desires, they lure back into sin those who have barely escaped from a lifestyle of deception. They promise freedom, but they themselves are slaves of sin and corruption. For you are a slave to whatever controls you. And when people escape from the wickedness of the world by knowing our Lord and Savior Jesus Christ and then get tangled up and enslaved by sin again, they are worse off than before. It would be better if they had never known the way to righteousness than to know it and then reject the command they were given to live a holy life."

We must learn to let go of our fears; we have been set free from fear. Therefore, we cannot allow it to control us.

- 2 Timothy 1:7–9 (NLT)—"For God has not given us a spirit of fear and timidity, but of power, love, and self-discipline. So never be ashamed to tell others about our Lord. And don't be ashamed of me, either, even though I'm in prison for him. With the strength God gives you, be ready to suffer with me for the sake of the Good News. For God saved us and called us to live a holy life. He did this, not because we deserved it, but because that was his plan from before the beginning of time—to show us his grace through Christ Jesus."

We must learn to let go of man-made religion and allow the Holy Spirit to teach us.

-Matthew 23:23–28 (NLT)—"What sorrow awaits you teachers of religious law and you Pharisees. Hypocrites! For you are careful to tithe even the tiniest income from your herb gardens, but you ignore the more important aspects of the law—justice, mercy, and faith. You should tithe, yes, but do not neglect the more important things. Blind guides! You strain your water so you won't accidentally swallow a gnat, but you swallow a camel! What sorrow awaits you teachers of religious law and you Pharisees. Hypocrites! For you are so careful to clean the outside of the cup and the dish, but inside you are filthy—full of greed and self-indulgence! You blind Pharisee! First wash the inside of the cup and the dish, and then the outside will become clean, too. What sorrow awaits you teachers of religious law and you Pharisees. Hypocrites! For you are like whitewashed tombs—beautiful on the

outside but filled on the inside with dead people's bones and all sorts of impurity. Outwardly you look like righteous people, but inwardly your hearts are filled with hypocrisy and lawlessness."

Learning to let go of our thinking and our desired lifestyle is one of the hardest things to do. Sadly, we desire for God to bless us in our own thinking, rather than for us to conform to His thinking. But He is God and not human like us. He is in control, not us. He is the master planner, not us. He foresees the future, not us. There is joy and peace in learning to let go and totally surrender ourselves to God the Father and our Lord Christ Jesus. We cannot think that we can partake of this world and still receive the blessings of God. He commands us to separate ourselves and not seek the riches of this world; it is all fading away! We must put our trust and desires on things that are from above and not in what we see. We have to let it all go so God can pour more of His Spirit into us.

Learning to Always Do Good and Put Others First: I believe the second hardest thing to accomplish that God requires in a true believer, is learning to put others before ourselves. There are very few people who would sacrifice their own money, time, and things, to see that the needs of others are being met before their own. There are a few who would share with others after they have achieved success, but not before their personal agenda is met. Because of His great wisdom, God knew that requesting us to put others first would require us to grow and separate ourselves from this world to accomplish His commandment.

> *- 2 Corinthians 6:17–18 (KJV) reads, "'Wherefore come out from among them, and be ye separate, saith the Lord, and touch not the unclean thing; and I will receive you, and will be a Father unto you, and ye shall be my sons and daughters,' saith the Lord Almighty."*

Putting others first is not easy, but it's a part of the transformation process to achieve maturity in Christ.

    - James 3:17–18 (NLT)—"But the wisdom from above is first of all pure. It is also peace loving, gentle at all times, and willing to yield to others. It is full of mercy and good deeds. It shows no favoritism and is always sincere. And those who are peacemakers will plant seeds of peace and reap a harvest of righteousness."

Doing good works is acceptable to God, but it will not cover up the sin from within.

    - James 3:13–16 (NLT)—"If you are wise and understand God's ways, prove it by living an honorable life, doing good works with the humility that comes from wisdom. But if you are bitterly jealous and there is selfish ambition in your heart, don't cover up the truth with boasting and lying. For jealousy and selfishness are not God's kind of wisdom. Such things are earthly, unspiritual, and demonic. For wherever there is jealousy and selfish ambition, there you will find disorder and evil of every kind."

We must take care of the poor, widows, and orphans, is required to accomplish true religion.

    - James 1:27 (NIV)—"Religion that God our Father accepts as pure and faultless is this: to look after orphans and widows in their distress and to keep oneself from being polluted by the world."

We must Take care of those who are weak and being commended for doing good work for Christ.

    - Romans 15:1–4 (NIV)—"We who are strong ought to bear with the failings of the weak and not to please ourselves. Each of us should please his neighbor for his good, to build him up. For even Christ did not please himself but, as it is written: 'The insults of those who insult you have fallen on me.' For everything that was written in the past was written to teach us, so that through endurance and the encouragement of the Scriptures we might have hope."

Spiritual Transformation

Many of us work hard every day doing just the opposite of what God is commanding us to do in producing for His kingdom. We look out for ourselves, and sometimes we masquerade our selfish desires as being the work of God. But God is teaching us not to cover up the real person on the inside by boasting about our works on the outside. We must be transformed to the point that both the inside of the cup and the outside of the cup are acceptable to God the Father and our Lord Jesus Christ.

Learning to Always Give God all the Glory: I believe there are only a few things that God requires us to do: 1) Accept His Word and be obedient to His Word. 2) Accept His son Christ Jesus and be obedient to Jesus Christ. 3) Accept His Holy Spirit, and be obedient to his teachings. 4) Become Holy, because God is holy. 5) Give God all the glory for saving us, blessing us in every way, and teaching us His ways. This means we do not accept someone telling us how great we are, but, instead, we tell them how great God is. We cannot allow people to put us on a pedestal; we must tell them how good God is. We cannot accept more than we need; we must allow our overflow to be used for God's purpose and His people. We work to ensure that all the glory is returned to God so He will see our humble spirit and bless us to serve Him more.

> *- 1 Peter 5:5–7 (NIV)—"All of you, clothe yourselves with humility toward one another, because, 'God opposes the proud but gives grace to the humble.' Humble yourselves, therefore, under God's mighty hand, that he may lift you up in due time. Cast all your anxiety on him because he cares for you."*

There is rest for us who are found standing in the shadow of God.

> *- Psalms 91:1 (NLT)—"Those who live in the shelter of the Most High will find rest in the shadow of the Almighty."*

Without guidance from the Holy Spirit, all of our plans are considered boasting of our own abilities.

Spiritual Transformation

- James 4:13–16 (NLT)—"Look here, you who say, 'Today or tomorrow we are going to a certain town and will stay there a year. We will do business there and make a profit.' How do you know what your life will be like tomorrow? Your life is like the morning fog—it's here a little while, then it's gone. What you ought to say is, 'If the Lord wants us to, we will live and do this or that.' Otherwise you are boasting about your own plans, and all such boasting is evil."

Because God has blessed us with all kinds of heavenly gifts, we should glorify Him in everything we do.

-1 Peter 4:10–11 (NLT)—"God has given each of you a gift from his great variety of spiritual gifts. Use them well to serve one another. Do you have the gift of speaking? Then speak as though God himself were speaking through you. Do you have the gift of helping others? Do it with all the strength and energy that God supplies. Then everything you do will bring glory to God through Jesus Christ. All glory and power to him forever and ever!"

Giving God all the glory is not something we do only with our lips, we should give Him all the glory by the way we live. We need to glorify God with our mind, body, and spirit. Anything short of praising Him with our whole being means we are boasting about our own capabilities.

Learning to Fear God: I have to be honest with you; I did not understand the concept of fearing God before He took the time to explain it to me. We need to comprehend how much God truly loves us and how perfect His plan is for us. We must believe with all our heart, soul, and being that He is in control and He is perfect.

God requires all His children to fear Him so we will hold on to his perfect ways and be loved by Him.

- Deuteronomy 10:12–15 (NLT)—"And now, Israel, what does the Lord your God require of you? He requires only that you fear the Lord your God, and live in a way that pleases him, and love him and serve him with all your heart and soul. And you must always obey the Lord's commands and decrees that I am giving you

today for your own good. Look, the highest heavens and the earth and everything in it all belong to the Lord your God."

Fearing God helps us to resist sinning. One of the main reasons God requires us to learn to fear Him is to keep us from sinning.

- Exodus 20:20 (NIV)—"Moses said to the people, 'Do not be afraid. God has come to test you, so that the fear of God will be with you to keep you from sinning.'

Learning to fear God allows us to cleanse ourselves from being defiled and to complete our assignment of becoming holy.

- 2 Corinthians 7:1 (NLT)—"Because we have these promises, dear friends, let us cleanse ourselves from everything that can defile our body or spirit. And let us work toward complete holiness because we fear God."

The time is coming when God will reveal everything we have done in the dark and behind closed doors. We must fear God because He has the power to destroy our very soul.

- Luke 12:2-5 (NLT)—"The time is coming when everything that is covered up will be revealed, and all that is secret will be made known to all. Whatever you have said in the dark will be heard in the light, and what you have whispered behind closed doors will be shouted from the housetops for all to hear! Dear friends, don't be afraid of those who want to kill your body; they cannot do any more to you after that. But I'll tell you whom to fear. Fear God, who has the power to kill you and then throw you into hell. Yes, he's the one to fear."

We must complete the preparation process so we can reach maturity in Christ. Even if we have to start over to get it correct, that would be better than living and teaching what is wrong as if it is the Word of God and then losing all that we have worked so long and hard to achieve.

- Hebrews 5:11–14 (NLT)—"There is much more we would like to say about this, but it is difficult to explain, especially since you are spiritually dull and don't seem to listen. You have been believers so long now that you ought to be teaching others. Instead, you

need someone to teach you again the basic things about God's word. You are like babies who need milk and cannot eat solid food. For someone who lives on milk is still an infant and doesn't know how to do what is right. Solid food is for those who are mature, who through training have the skill to recognize the difference between right and wrong."

Growing Through Spiritual Transformation

Once we have received the Holy Spirit and established our relationship with God the Father and Christ Jesus, the Holy Spirit can start teaching us how to grow during our transformation process. We have learned how to love God with all our heart, body, soul, and spirit. There is nothing that we attempt to do without first approaching God and seeking His direction and instructions. Most all the time we spend in the transformation process stage is focused on getting us right with God and Christ Jesus. We should spend very little time going out and teaching others about God because He is preparing us for service. Many times, people in the transformation process will try and jump right to the growing stage of transformation. When this happens, many times these individuals have to go back and start over again in the transformation process stage. Paul spoke about this in the following scripture. (1 Corinthians 3:2–6)

No Turning Back: Once God has directed and instructed us to move forward and go out and teach, preach, and be a voice for the Lord, there is no turning back. We now know what the Spirit of the Lord is about and the power that comes through a divine relationship with God the Father and Jesus Christ. If we decide to turn back, there are grave consequences.

Jesus teaches us that we cannot take our hands off the plow and turn back.

- Luke 9:62 (NLT)—"But Jesus told him, 'Anyone who puts a hand to the plow and then looks back is not fit for the Kingdom of God.'"

We have to be very careful. Once we have walked with God and experienced His goodness, we cannot reject Him.

> *- Hebrews 6:4–6 (NLT)—"For it is impossible to bring back to repentance those who were once enlightened—those who have experienced the good things of heaven and shared in the Holy Spirit, who have tasted the goodness of the word of God and the power of the age to come—and who then turn away from God. It is impossible to bring such people back to repentance; by rejecting the Son of God, they themselves are nailing him to the cross once again and holding him up to public shame."*

Once we have given our lives over to God the Father and Jesus Christ, we cannot go back and start doing the things we use to do; Jesus will judge us and assign us a place with the unbelievers.

> *- Luke 12:45–48 (NIV)—"But suppose the servant says to himself, 'My master is taking a long time in coming,' and he then begins to beat the menservants and maidservants and to eat and drink and get drunk. The master of that servant will come on a day when he does not expect him and at an hour he is not aware of. He will cut him to pieces and assign him a place with the unbelievers. That servant who knows his master's will and does not get ready or does not do what his master wants will be beaten with many blows. But the one who does not know and does things deserving punishment will be beaten with few blows. From everyone who has been given much, much will be demanded; and from he one who has been entrusted with much, much more will be asked."*

Fit for Service: God the Father and our Lord Christ Jesus is preparing us for service in the kingdom of God. We must be declared ready and fit for service. We are taught to put on the whole armor of God so we can stand and endure.

We must work each and every day to prove that we are ready to receive Christ Jesus when he returns. We have to remain dressed for service, awaiting our reward. (Luke 12:35–38)

Part of being ready and fit for service is to have self-control of our mind and body. We must be able to always think clearly, so we can live in obedience to achieve holiness. (1 Peter 1:13–16)

Those who are prepared for service can have confidence, that God has a plan for them.

- Jeremiah 29:11–13 (NIV)—"'For I know the plans I have for you,' declares the Lord, 'plans to prosper you and not to harm you, plans to give you hope and a future. Then you will call upon me and come and pray to me, and I will listen to you. You will seek me and find me when you seek me with all your heart."

We must grow so we are freed from this world, sinful nature, and Satan. As we continue to grow and allow the Holy Spirit to change our nature, we should start seeing a change in ourselves. This change should show up in the way we look at this world and everything in it. We have to become free and remain free so we can serve God to carry out His plan and not our own. (Colossians 2:20–23)

As we grow, it's important that we are living by the Spirit.

- Galatians 5:24–26 (NLT)—"Those who belong to Christ Jesus have nailed the passions and desires of their sinful nature to his cross and crucified them there. Since we are living by the Spirit, let us follow the Spirit's leading in every part of our lives. Let us not become conceited, or provoke one another, or be jealous of one another."

Because we are living and being directed by the Spirit of God, we must count all other desires and motives as garbage.

- Philippians 3:7–11 (NLT)—"I once thought these things were valuable, but now I consider them worthless because of what Christ has done. Yes, everything else is worthless when compared with the infinite value of knowing Christ Jesus my Lord. For his sake I have discarded everything else, counting it all as garbage, so that I could gain Christ and become one with him. I no longer count on my own righteousness through obeying the law; rather, I become righteous through faith in Christ. For God's way of making us right with himself depends on faith. I want to know

Christ and experience the mighty power that raised him from the dead. I want to suffer with him, sharing in his death, so that one way or another I will experience the resurrection from the dead!"

To remain free once God wipes all our sins away is a struggle for all Christians. Satan is looking to destroy all of us who have placed our trust and hope in God the Father and our Lord Jesus Christ. The longer we remain free, the more we should experience God's presence. We should become confident in Christ Jesus and in his willingness to help us as we struggle and overcome. In Revelation, Jesus lets us know that he understands our struggles to remain free and to avoid getting re-tangled in this world. (Revelation 2:9–10)

As God's Holy Spirit prepares us for His service, we are wiped clean from all our sins. We must allow our spirit to remain free from all that binds us so we can receive all that God has for us. We are to work to keep all of our hopes, thoughts, and desires before God so we are counted fit for service.

Called into Service by God: Once we place our trust in God the Father and our Lord Jesus Christ and after we are prepared to walk in God's truths, we are freed from our sins. God decides when to call us into service. I believe many times God reveals to us ahead of time His plan for us to serve Him. Unfortunately, we may decide that we are tired of being in the preparation stage and jump into doing what God has revealed to us. We must not decide when or where God is calling us into service. We must allow God to complete the work He is doing in us so that, when we are called into service, every step we take is ordered by God. If we jump ship and start making up our own plan to accomplish what God has revealed, it will, in most cases, eventually fail. For many of us, there is still a great deal of bad desires and behaviors that remain in our body even after we become saved and God has forgiven us and wiped away all our past sins. If we don't fully complete the preparation stage, some of those bad desires and habits will come back and generate sin in our lives. Once that happens, we can choose to hide them or we can go back and allow God's Holy Spirit to complete the preparation stage. Most of the time, we will not choose to reenter the preparation stage, and God has to allow that sin to be revealed.

Unfortunately, we may already be a pastor or a religious leader when this happens, so we suffer a great fall. If we allow God's Holy Spirit to complete its work, God will prepare us for a great service. We must not begin to order our own steps and take back control over our life after we have surrendered it to God for His service. If we do, then our relationship with God the Father and our Lord Jesus Christ will suffer. And, if we totally turn away from God after experiencing God's love and acceptance, we will be in danger of losing our salvation.

Being called for God's purpose: We must understand that our calling is for God's purpose and not our own. So many times you see those who are called working to produce for their own purpose. But, in Romans, God is calling us for His purpose because He chose us to live in right standing with Him.

> *- Romans 8:27–30 (NLT)—"And the Father who knows all hearts knows what the Spirit is saying, for the Spirit pleads for us believers in harmony with God's own will. And we know that God causes everything to work together for the good of those who love God and are called according to his purpose for them. For God knew his people in advance, and he chose them to become like his Son, so that his Son would be the firstborn among many brothers and sisters. And having chosen them, he called them to come to him. And having called them, he gave them right standing with himself."*

When God calls us by name: I can tell you there is no greater experience and enlightenment than when God the Father and our Lord Jesus Christ call's us by our name. If you look at the prophets and apostles in the Bible, those whom God called by name knew actually what God wanted from them. When God grants us grace and we are obedient to God's will, our relationship with God will grow. In Exodus, God speaks directly to Moses and gives Moses confidence.

> *- Exodus 33:17–19 (KJV)—"And the LORD said unto Moses, I will do this thing also that thou hast spoken: for thou hast found grace*

in my sight, and I know thee by name. And he said, I beseech thee, shew me thy glory. And he said, I will make all my goodness pass before thee, and I will proclaim the name of the LORD before thee; and will be gracious to whom I will be gracious, and will shew mercy on whom I will shew mercy."

Being fully persuaded when we are called: One of the most important aspects we must maintain regarding being called into service, is our ability to stay fully persuaded that we are called to do God's will. Many times, after years have gone by, we become complacent in our work for God. We may even start performing work that is not directed by God, but we label it as doing God's work. This is why we are taught the importance of being renewed each day by the Holy Spirit so we take on nothing that is not directed by God. We must remain fully persuaded of our calling and purpose. Nothing should be able to move us from our calling, as Paul shares in Romans.

- Romans 8:37–39 (NKJV)—"Yet in all these things we are more than conquerors through Him who loved us. For I am persuaded that neither death nor life, nor angels nor principalities nor powers, nor things present nor things to come, nor height nor depth, nor any other created thing, shall be able to separate us from the love of God which is in Christ Jesus our Lord."

Working in God's vineyard: We must not become confused about the work we are being called to do. God is not calling us to work in His vineyard to build buildings, generate wealth, obtain things in this world, or for us to be glorified by others. Those who are called into service are called to teach God's people his truth and ways and to preach the Good News. We are called to bring souls to Christ, to uplift the poor, to take care of the widows, and to help rescue those who are lost. The work in God's vineyard is hard because we have to deal with people and their situations and circumstances, however, that is the work God is calling us to do. It is not self-gratifying, and it's not self-seeking; it's all to give God the glory. (Luke 10:2–3)

Spiritual Transformation

Producing for God: The outcome of being called into service is to produce for God's people and to return all the glory to God. That means, as God provides a means for us to produce, we won't accept any of the glory or store up any of the wealth. We must learn how to be directed by God's voice and be in complete obedience to His will. Any deviation from His plan will get us into worldly thinking, which only brings us glory if we are somehow successful. Jesus warns us about this type of thinking in (Matthew 7:21).

God is not interested in our plan; He is interested in us carrying out His plan. As we begin to produce, based on God's plan, we will see God the Father and Jesus Christ working to bring His plan to completion. (John 5:16–17)

Producing from our calling: Once we understand and become clear on God's purpose and calling for us, we can now produce. God defines the way we should produce for him. There are two things that should happen as a result of us producing for God: 1) having the ability to be generous to others and 2) those who are helped being joyful and expressing thanks to God. God is producing in us for the sole purpose of us being generous to others and not building up wealth for ourselves and storing it up.

> *- 2 Corinthians 9:10–12 (NLT)—"For God is the one who provides seed for the farmer and then bread to eat. In the same way, he will provide and increase your resources and then produce a great harvest of generosity in you. Yes, you will be enriched in every way so that you can always be generous. And when we take your gifts to those who need them, they will thank God. So two good things will result from this ministry of giving—the needs of the believers in Jerusalem will be met, and they will joyfully express their thanks to God."*

Learning directly from Christ Jesus and God the Father: It's important that we allow God and the Holy Spirit to direct and order our steps. If we try to order our own steps and create a plan hoping for God to bless it, we will end up walking in disobedience. God wants to order our steps based on His purpose of us. In Psalms, David is calling out to God to order his steps and to teach him all of God's ways. (Psalms 119:132–135)

David knew what it meant to be outside of God's will. The more and more we come to know God the Father and our Lord Jesus Christ, the better we will be in following His direction and pleasing Him in our work for His Kingdom.

> *- Colossians 1:9–10 (NLT)—"We ask God to give you complete knowledge of his will and to give you spiritual wisdom and understanding. Then the way you live will always honor and please the Lord, and your lives will produce every kind of good fruit. All the while, you will grow as you learn to know God better and better."*

Being able to see God and Christ Jesus at work: As we learn to work from God's plan and God directs our steps, we will see the effects of our obedience in others. They will see the Spirit of God at work in us, and we will be able to tell them just how great the love of God is. We will be able to demonstrate what it means to live in God's will and produce a harvest for His vineyard. Paul shares with us an expectation of pleasing God by growing in our salvation. (Philippians 2:12–13)

Becoming un-teachable: As God starts to use us to produce, we must not become un-teachable. We must not become self-righteous in our thinking. Just because we have experienced the power of God in our service to Him does not mean God will remain with us if we fall away. There are many stories in the Bible where God had no choice but to abandon His chosen leaders because they stopped seeking God and turned to their own knowledge and wisdom. Saul is a perfect example. God chose Saul, but Saul decided he was not going to wait on Samuel to anoint him as King. Saul decided to take this upon himself. After Saul had implemented several of his own plans, God decided to take the kingdom from Saul because he did not fully obey God's instructions. Saul decided to carry some of the plunder back and give it to his men after God had instructed him to destroy it all. Saul thought he was in God's will, but changing even a part little of God's plan can take us out of His will and cost us dearly. We must always listen to God's voice and never change, add, or modify God's Word, plan, or purpose. The key to staying teachable is humility. If we can keep self-righteousness, pride, arrogance, and creative thinking, out of our spirit, we can maintain humility and allow the Holy Spirit to teach and direct us.

> *- 2 Timothy 3:16–17 (NLT)—"All Scripture is inspired by God and is useful to teach us what is true and to make us realize what is wrong in our lives. It corrects us when we are wrong and teaches us to do what is right. God uses it to prepare and equip his people to do every good work."*

Guided by the Holy Spirit: As mentioned before, without the Holy Spirit, we cannot enter into the preparation process. I will take that even further by saying that, without God's Holy Spirit, we cannot remain in His presence and under His grace. God has assigned the Holy Spirit to be our guide. There are so many teachings out there about the Holy Spirit and how one receives it. This seems to be a good time to review what God's plan is regarding receiving the Holy Spirit and its purpose.

God's Spirit at the Beginning: From the beginning of time, God covered the earth with his Holy Spirit. It is the presence of God's Spirit that allows things to occur on earth. It is pointed out in Genesis that God's Spirit hovered over the earth. (Genesis 1:1–2)

We then come to understand that God decided to remove His Spirit because of the sin in man.

> *- Genesis 6:3 (KJV)—"And the LORD said, My spirit shall not always strive with man, for that he also is flesh: yet his days shall be an hundred and twenty years." We can see that God planned for His presence to remain with man, but our actions made God adjust His plan to deal with man's ways.*

God's Spirit enables us to complete His plan: We can see that from the beginning God placed His Spirit in man to enable His plan to be completed.

- Exodus 31:1–5 (KJV)—"And the LORD spake unto Moses, saying, 'See, I have called by name Bezaleel the son of Uri, the son of Hur, of the tribe of Judah: And I have filled him with the spirit of God, in wisdom, and in understanding, and in knowledge, and in all manner of workmanship, to devise cunning works, to work in gold, and in silver, and in brass, and in cutting of stones, to set them, and in carving of timber, to work in all manner of workmanship.'"

God would also take His Spirit and place it on others so they could become a part of God's work.

- Numbers 11:16–17 (NIV)—"The Lord said to Moses: 'Bring me seventy of Israel's elders who are known to you as leaders and officials among the people. Have them come to the Tent of Meeting, that they may stand there with you. I will come down and speak with you there, and I will take of the Spirit that is on you and put the Spirit on them. They will help you carry the burden of the people so that you will not have to carry it alone.'" God takes His same Spirit and shares it with others, so we can be like-minded in doing God's work.

The purpose of the Holy Spirit is to enable us to do God's work, to teach us God's ways, and to gather us together.

- Isaiah 34:16–17 (NIV)—"None of these will be missing, not one will lack her mate. For it is his mouth that has given the order, and his Spirit will gather them together. He allots their portions; his hand distributes them by measure."

God the Father then placed His Spirit into Jesus Christ; this was prophesied in Isaiah.

- Isaiah 42:1–4 (KJV)—"Behold my servant, whom I uphold; mine elect, in whom my soul delighteth; I have put my spirit upon him: he shall bring forth judgment to the Gentiles. He shall not cry, nor lift up, nor cause his voice to be heard in the street. A bruised reed shall he not break, and the smoking flax shall he not quench: he shall bring forth judgment unto truth. He shall not fail nor be discouraged, till he have set judgment in the earth: and the isles shall wait for his law."

And we see these prophecies come true in Matthew.

> - Matthew 3:16–17 (KJV)—"And Jesus, when he was baptized, went up straightway out of the water: and, lo, the heavens were opened unto him, and he saw the Spirit of God descending like a dove, and lighting upon him: And lo a voice from heaven, saying,
>
> 'This is my beloved Son, in whom I am well pleased.'" Now, God's Spirit rests with man through our belief in His Son Christ Jesus.

Receiving the Holy Spirit: As we can see, God Himself can cause His Spirit to come upon a man. Another way a person can receive the Holy Spirit is by a person who has the Holy Spirit laying their hands on another person. In Deuteronomy, Moses lays his hands on Joshua so God would fill him with the Holy Spirit. (Deuteronomy 34:9)

Again, in 2 Kings 2:15 (KJV), Elijah's spirit was passed on to Elisha. A key process in receiving the Holy Spirit is the process of being born again. Without this process occurring in our lives, we cannot enter into the Kingdom of God. (John 3:5–7)

It's important that we receive the Holy Spirit because, without it, we cannot worship God correctly, for God is Spirit and we must worship Him in spirit.

> - John 4:23–24 (NLT)—"But the time is coming—indeed it's here now—when true worshipers will worship the Father in spirit and in truth. The Father is looking for those who will worship him that way. For God is Spirit, so those who worship him must worship in spirit and in truth."

By us receiving and maintaining the Holy Spirit in us, we can receive eternal life.

> - John 6:63–64 (NLT)—"The Spirit alone gives eternal life. Human effort accomplishes nothing. And the very words I have spoken to you are spirit and life. But some of you do not believe me."

For those who love Christ Jesus and obey his commandments, Jesus will give us the Holy Spirit to lead us into God's truth.

- John 14:15–17 (NLT)—"If you love me, obey my commandments. And I will ask the Father, and he will give you another Advocate, who will never leave you. He is the Holy Spirit, who leads into all truth. The world cannot receive him, because it isn't looking for him and doesn't recognize him. But you know him, because he lives with you now and later will be in you."

Jesus Christ passed the Holy Spirit on to His disciples by breathing upon them.

- John 20:22–23 (NLT)—"Then he breathed on them and said, 'Receive the Holy Spirit. If you forgive anyone's sins, they are forgiven. If you do not forgive them, they are not forgiven.'"

Another way we can receive God's Holy Spirit is through baptism.

- Acts 1:4–5 (NLT)—"Once when he was eating with them, he commanded them, 'Do not leave Jerusalem until the Father sends you the gift he promised, as I told you before. John baptized with water, but in just a few days you will be baptized with the Holy Spirit.'"

Receiving the Holy Spirit is not about what you can obtain. Many times, God's Spirit may lead us into the wilderness or direct us in a way that is not according to our plan, but we must remain obedient to what the Holy Spirit is telling us to do. We must see our lives as being worth nothing without the Holy Spirit guiding us and completing the work we are called to do. (Acts 20:22–24)

The evidence of receiving the Holy Spirit is having a changed heart. The Holy Spirit works inside of us to change our hearts to seek and praise God and not man.

- Romans 2:29 (NLT)—"No, a true Jew is one whose heart is right with God. And true circumcision is not merely obeying the letter of the law; rather, it is a change of heart produced by God's Spirit. And a person with a changed heart seeks praise from God, not from people."

Spiritual Transformation

Paul teaches us that it is not by clever and persuasive words that we demonstrate God's presence when we preach or teach the Word of God but by the power of the Holy Spirit. (Corinthians 2:4)

Paul goes on to teach us that, by having the Holy Spirit, we will be able to use spiritual words to explain spiritual truths. Not everyone can hear what the Spirit has to say, so they cannot understand the secrets of God. (1 Corinthians 2:13–15)
By the power of the Holy Spirit: We learn that Jesus Christ has the power to cast out demons because he is stronger than Satan. (Matthew 12:28–29)

We are taught that by the Holy Spirit that we are equipped to speak the right words at the right time and that the Holy Spirit helps us to overcome fear.

> *-Mark 13:11 (NLT)*—*"But when you are arrested and stand trial, don't worry in advance about what to say. Just say what God tells you at that time, for it is not you who will be speaking, but the Holy Spirit."*

It is through God's Holy Spirit that miracles occur in our lives, as in the days of Mary and Elizabeth.

> *- Luke 1:34–36 (NLT)*—*"Mary asked the angel, 'But how can this happen? I am a virgin.' The angel replied, 'The Holy Spirit will come upon you, and the power of the Most High will overshadow you. So the baby to be born will be holy, and he will be called the Son of God. What's more, your relative Elizabeth has become pregnant in her old age!'"*

I believe one of the amazing powers the Holy Spirit is his ability to reveal and direct our ways.

> *- Luke 2:25–27 (NLT)*—*"At that time there was a man in Jerusalem named Simeon. He was righteous and devout and was eagerly waiting for the Messiah to come and rescue Israel. The Holy Spirit was upon him and had revealed to him that he would not die until he had seen the Lord's Messiah. That day the Spirit led him to the Temple."*

Spiritual Transformation

God's Spirit allows us to know the truth and the ability to teach and preach the Good News, and he grants us favor.

> - *Luke 4:18–19 (NLT)—"The Spirit of the Lord is upon me, for he has anointed me to bring Good News to the poor. He has sent me to proclaim that captives will be released, that the blind will see, that the oppressed will be set free, and that the time of the Lord's favor has come."*

When we receive the Holy Spirit, it will teach us all that God the Father and Jesus Christ has for us to know. The Holy Spirit will teach us about the future and how to give God all the glory and honor.

> - *John 16:13–15 (NLT)—"When the Spirit of truth comes, he will guide you into all truth. He will not speak on his own but will tell you what he has heard. He will tell you about the future. He will bring me glory by telling you whatever he receives from me. All that belongs to the Father is mine; this is why I said, 'The Spirit will tell you whatever he receives from me.'"*

When Jesus sent the Holy Spirit upon his disciples in Acts, the Holy Spirit enabled them to communicate God's Word with others, by speaking in their language.

> - *Acts 2:3–4 (NLT) —"Then, what looked like flames or tongues of fire appeared and settled on each of them. And everyone present was filled with the Holy Spirit and began speaking in other languages, as the Holy Spirit gave them this ability."*

These days, there are many churches being established daily, it's important that we understand that only through the Holy Spirit can a church really grow in a way that is pleasing to God.

> - *Acts 9:31 (NLT)—"The church then had peace throughout Judea, Galilee, and Samaria, and it became stronger as the believers lived in the fear of the Lord. And with the encouragement of the Holy Spirit, it also grew in numbers."*

Healing is another area where the power of the Holy Spirit is manifested. We know that Jesus performed many acts of healing and cured the sick. Healing is a gift from the Holy Spirit, as demonstrated with Ananias and Paul.

> - Acts 9:17–18 (NLT)—"So Ananias went and found Saul. He laid his hands on him and said, 'Brother Saul, the Lord Jesus, who appeared to you on the road, has sent me so that you might regain your sight and be filled with the Holy Spirit.' Instantly something like scales fell from Saul's eyes, and he regained his sight."

Another Gift of the Holy Spirit is the ability to see visions. I believe this allows those whom God has chosen to see the future and help lead God's people.

> - Acts 10:19–20 (NLT)—"Meanwhile, as Peter was puzzling over the vision, the Holy Spirit said to him, 'Three men have come looking for you. Get up, go downstairs, and go with them without hesitation. Don't worry, for I have sent them.'"

Still another gift from the Holy Spirit is the ability to prophesy over demons, as when Paul dealt with the sorcerer in Acts.

> - Acts 13:9–11 (NLT)—"Saul, also known as Paul, was filled with the Holy Spirit, and he looked the sorcerer in the eye. Then he said, 'You son of the devil, full of every sort of deceit and fraud, and enemy of all that is good! Will you never stop perverting the true ways of the Lord? Watch now, for the Lord has laid his hand of punishment upon you, and you will be struck blind. You will not see the sunlight for some time.'"

One incredible gift that the Holy Spirit provides to some is the ability to raise a person from the dead. We know that God raised Jesus from the dead by His Holy Spirit. (Romans 1:2–4)

This world has taught us one way of expressing love to each other, which is based on us receiving something in return for our love. But God's love is not based on what He receives from us, and the only way we can obtain this type of love is through God's Holy Spirit.

> - Romans 5:5 (NLT)—"For we know how dearly God loves us, because he has given us the Holy Spirit to fill our hearts with his love."

Now that we have been taught to love as God loves us, we become free to allow God's Spirit to control our mind so we can please God.

> - Romans 8:5–6 (NLT)—"Those who are dominated by the sinful nature think about sinful things, but those who are controlled by
>
> the Holy Spirit think about things that please the Spirit. So letting your sinful nature control your mind leads to death. But letting the Spirit control your mind leads to life and peace."

For we must allow God's Spirit to work with our spirit to put to death all the sinful deeds that remain in our body. By going through this process, we become children of God.

> - Romans 8:13–14 (NLT)—"For if you live by its dictates, you will die. But if through the power of the Spirit you put to death the deeds of your sinful nature, you will live. For all who are led by the Spirit of God are children of God. So you have not received a spirit that makes you fearful slaves. Instead, you received God's Spirit when he adopted you as his own children. Now we call him, 'Abba, Father.' For his Spirit joins with our spirit to affirm that we are God's children."

We also learn that the Holy Spirit helps us in our weakness; it takes on the responsibility of praying for us when we are weak. In our ignorance, we don't know what we should be praying for, so God's Spirit intercedes for us with groaning that only the Father can understand, to bring us into harmony with His will.

> - Romans 8:26–27 (NLT)—"And the Holy Spirit helps us in our weakness. For example, we don't know what God wants us to pray for. But the Holy Spirit prays for us with groanings that cannot be expressed in words. And the Father who knows all hearts knows what the Spirit is saying, for the Spirit pleads for us believers in harmony with God's own will."

Spiritual Transformation

We have to believe that we were made holy and in right standing with God when we called on the name of our Lord Jesus Christ and we received God's Holy Spirit.

> - 1 Corinthians 6:11 (NLT)—"But you were cleansed; you were made holy; you were made right with God by calling on the name of the Lord Jesus Christ and by the Spirit of our God."

It is the responsibility of the Holy Spirit to distribute what God has instructed him to do and impart gifts unto us so we can help one another. The Holy Spirit decides, based on God's purpose, which person gets which gifts, for God has assigned the Holy Spirit this task.

> - 1 Corinthians 12:7–11 (NLT)—"A spiritual gift is given to each of us so we can help each other. To one person the Spirit gives the ability to give wise advice; to another the same Spirit gives a message of special knowledge. The same Spirit gives great faith to another, and to someone else the one Spirit gives the gift of healing. He gives one person the power to perform miracles, and another the ability to prophesy. He gives someone else the ability to discern whether a message is from the Spirit of God or from another spirit. Still another person is given the ability to speak in unknown languages, while another is given the ability to interpret what is being said. It is the one and only Spirit who distributes all these gifts. He alone decides which gift each person should have."

There are many teachings about the purpose of speaking in tongues or in another language, but this in itself is not an indication that God's Spirit is with anyone, for if we don't have Godly love, we are not from God, for God is love. We also understand that it is better to prophesy than to speak in tongues to those who cannot understand what is being said. If we speak in tongues, we are only speaking to God, but the power of prophesying strengthens others and the entire church. (1 Corinthians 14:1–4)

Finally, we must become spiritual because God is Spirit. And we learn through the Spirit of God, which is on the inside of us, how to become free. I believe the greatest gift of the Holy Spirit while we remain on this earth is for us to be free from all the trials and troubles that come from trying to live on earth pleasing ourselves. The veil is lifted so we can clearly see what God has for us and see our purpose in life. (2 Corinthians 3:16–18)

In our freedom, we work to prove ourselves by the way we live. Through the Holy Spirit, we gain Godly understanding, patience, and kindness. The Holy Spirit also teaches us how to have sincere love for God and others. We must remain faithful and allow God's power to work in us, using the weapons of righteousness in the right hand for attack and in the left hand for defense, for the very purpose of serving God, no matter how we are treated. (2 Corinthians 6:6–8)

Can we lose God's Spirit? Can we, through our actions and deeds, lose the Holy Spirit or cause it to leave us? We know that the actions of Saul caused the Holy Spirit to leave him. And David, in Psalms, cries out to God for the Holy Spirit to remain with him.

> *- Psalms 51:10–12 (KJV)—"Create in me a clean heart, O God; and renew a right spirit within me. Cast me not away from thy presence; and take not thy holy spirit from me. Restore unto me the joy of thy salvation; and uphold me with thy free spirit."*

We learn in Matthew that, if we commit blasphemy against God's Spirit, we cannot be forgiven for such a sin.

> *- Matthew 12:31 (NLT)—"Every sin and blasphemy can be forgiven—except blasphemy against the Holy Spirit, which will never be forgiven."*

Another way we can lose God's Holy Spirit is through our deceitfulness and allowing Satan to control us, as with Ananias.

> *-Acts 5:3–5 (NLT)—"Then Peter said, 'Ananias, why have you let Satan fill your heart? You lied to the Holy Spirit, and you kept some of the money for yourself. The property was yours to sell or not sell, as you wished. And after selling it, the money was also yours to give away. How could you do a thing like this? You weren't lying to us but to God!' As soon as Ananias heard these words, he fell to the floor and died."*

Spiritual Transformation

We know that the Spirit of God is on the inside of us to set us free. Its purpose is to get us transformed into the image of Christ. To do this, the Spirit of God has to clean us up and impart God's gifts to us so we can produce for Him. We have to be careful that we don't take our salvation lightly, for Satan is still looking to recapture those who have crossed over. We have to remain watchful over our spirit, words, works, and actions. We must be willing to allow the Holy Spirit to examine us from the inside and reveal everything in us that is not pleasing to God. We have to listen to what the Spirit of God is saying to us, for his purpose is to bring God glory through the renewing of our mind and spirit.

Continuously Walking and Praying in the Spirit: As we continue to grow in Christ with the Holy Spirit living on the inside of us, we must continue to walk in a way that returns all the glory to God. Walking with Christ will require us to give up everything to serve him. If we are looking to hold on to anything in this life, we are not worthy of the calling. We must remember the very words that Christ said in (Matthew 10:37–39)

Called to walk with Christ Jesus. I know there are many sermons being preached that say, once we have accepted Christ, we will receive prosperity and riches in this world. But the true work of Christ will bring about hard times, because working with people is the hardest job in the world. Paul encourages fellow believers in this work. (Acts 14:22)

We have to come to the understanding that walking with Christ means living without sin. We cannot assume that grace will allow us to live a life of sin as we call on the name of Jesus. We are fooling ourselves, as Paul states in (Romans 6:1–2).

Praying in the Spirit: Because we have the Spirit of God on the inside of us, we must learn to pray in the spirit. This does not come from observation of man, but from the teaching that comes from the Holy Spirit. No one can teach you how to pray in the Spirit; God through His Holy Spirit enables us to pray in the Spirit. We must remain watchful and have perseverance in our prayer life, praying for all who need prayer with all kinds of supplication.

Spiritual Transformation

- Ephesians 6:17–18 (NKJV)—*"And take the helmet of salvation, and the sword of the Spirit, which is the word of God; praying always with all prayer and supplication in the Spirit, being watchful to this end with all perseverance and supplication for all the saints."*

God's Grace and Mercy: As we continue to grow in Christ, God will extend His grace and mercy to those who are working to overcome. Jesus Christ is our High Priest, who understands all of our needs. God the Father placed everything under his feet— that includes you and I. Our relationship with Christ allows us to come boldly to the throne of God. At the throne of God, we will receive mercy and we will find grace to help us when we need it the most. (Hebrews 4:15–16)

Growing in spiritual integrity: As we complete the preparation stage and God calls us into service, we must maintain spiritual integrity. Others will be able to see Christ in us, in all situations and circumstances. Each and every day, we must walk clothed in the Spirit and in humility that comes from God. We must be able to walk in confidence that our salvation is secure in Christ Jesus. We must be an example by completing the good work that God has started in us. In everything we do, we must reflect integrity and maintain the seriousness of God's teaching in our lives; speaking the very truths of God so we cannot be criticized. (Titus 2:7–8)

As God completes His work in us, we should be removed from the cares of this world so nothing can entangle us back in to Satan's grasp. By now, we should be living to please God the Father and our Lord Jesus Christ. Therefore, we do not have a spirit that turns to the right or left; a spirit that turns back because of the cares of this world. We do not peddle God's Word to make a living off the backs of God's people. Those who are called by God, have no issue working with our hands so no one can find any fault in our teaching, which comes from God's Holy Spirit. Though God's leaders are allowed to partake of their living from the church, they don't do this in a way that causes others to stumble and fall. We are careful about our desires, and we keep ourselves in line with what pleases God. We do not create schemes for getting rich or storing up riches for ourselves. We work in every way to encourage, uplift, and suffer for the body of Christ; for this reason, we were called and chosen. We cannot mock God by covering up hidden desires and pleasures as if God does not see them. Instead, we are open and we spend time with the Holy Spirit to examine ourselves in the very presence of God's throne.

The Outcome of Spiritual Transformation

After we have been told by God that we have moved from the preparation stage and into the growth stage, we should experience some of the outcomes that come from being transformed into Christ's likeness. Because God will always be our Father and Jesus Christ will always be our Lord, we will always be learning from them and applying God's loving ways to our lives. Paul speaks of completing the race and completing his tasks, as a sign that he has completed the transformation process.

> - 2 Timothy 4:6–8 (NLT)—"As for me, my life has already been poured out as an offering to God. The time of my death is near. I have fought the good fight, I have finished the race, and I have remained faithful. And now the prize awaits me—the crown of righteousness, which the Lord, the righteous Judge, will give me on the day of his return. And the prize is not just for me but for all who eagerly look forward to his appearing."

Those who complete the transformation process will be changed. They will not look at life as a measure of their own success. Those who have been transformed look at success from what they have produced for God. They will not see themselves based on what they have collected and stored up but from the continuous giving that comes from a changed heart. They will not be seen as a person of human knowledge and human wisdom but as a person whose spirit is encapsulated in the very essence that comes from walking with God and being taught by the Holy Spirit. We, the transformed, must complete the race and follow in the footsteps of Jesus Christ, Paul, Peter, John, and other apostles and disciples of God. The whole goal of completing the transformation process is for God to grant us entry into His kingdom and for us to give God the Father and our Lord Jesus Christ all the glory! Amen.

Joy and Peace While on Earth: Peace on earth, what a sweet sounding idea. If we look at the world we live in, there is very little evidence of peace on earth. Is it even possible to imagine that people of other nations can one day get along and live in harmony? We cannot even get our own country to live in peace and harmony. The concept of a world living in peace is too far-reaching for us on this earth. If we read in Genesis, we will see that God set up the perfect environment for this to happen. God supplied everything we needed. All we had to do was allow him to be our God, but we did not follow God's will; we just had to continue to listen to the destructive forces on the inside of us. But, God did not give up on us. Instead, He gave us judges, prophets, and leaders to get us to accept His joy and peace, but we killed them all. God did not give up on us, so He sent His only Son to save us; but, we killed him, too. Still, God did not give up on us. He promised that if we as individuals would seek His face with all our heart and soul, He will be faithful and grant us joy and peace on earth through the precious blood of Christ Jesus.

> - *Romans 14:17–18 (NIV)—"For the kingdom of God is not a matter of eating and drinking, but of righteousness, peace and joy in the Holy Spirit, because anyone who serves Christ in this way is pleasing to God and approved by men."*

The plan that God had in Genesis is the same plan that is spoken of in Revelation concerning a new heaven and a new earth—all things will become new to fulfill God's plan from the beginning.

> - *Revelation 21:1–6 (NLT)—"Then I saw a new heaven and a new earth, for the old heaven and the old earth had disappeared. And the sea was also gone. And I saw the holy city, the new Jerusalem, coming down from God out of heaven like a bride beautifully dressed for her husband. I heard a loud shout from the throne, saying, 'Look, God's home is now among his people! He will live with them, and they will be his people. God himself will be with them. He will wipe every tear from their eyes, and there will be no more death or sorrow or crying or pain. All these things are*

gone forever.' And the one sitting on the throne said, 'Look, I am making everything new!' And then he said to me, 'Write this down, for what I tell you is trustworthy and true.' And he also said, 'It is finished! I am the Alpha and the Omega—the Beginning and the End.'"

So what was started from the beginning will be completed in the end.

The state of your soul: The world is constantly teaching us that what matters most, are the treasures that we build up on earth. What matters the most for those who have been transformed are the heavenly treasures that we build up in God the Father and our Lord Jesus Christ. Jesus warns us when he stated, "What does it matter to gain the whole world but lose your soul?" (Matthew 16:26–27)

There is an issue when we believe that it is necessary for us to become wealthy as we do the work God is calling us to perform. Is it not God who provides all our needs and supplies us with everything to do the work we are called to do? Isn't the first thing's God is calls us to do, is become saved, live our lives like Jesus, and seek Christ with all our heart and soul, so He will protect us? Does not God teach us that going after the cares of this world and seeking its riches, separates us from Him? But we still teach and encourage people to chase after the very things that will cause us to become disconnected from God. Is it worth it, to gain the whole world and lose our soul? Is it worth it, to gain all the riches of the world, and lose our soul? Is it worth it, to be praised by man and lose our soul? We must count the cost. (Luke 14:27–30)

Why would we allow God to start a good work in us and forfeit it to gain the world and the praises of man and lose our salvation? Our soul is worth much more than that!

Obtaining true happiness: I don't want you to think that I am against becoming prosperous; that is not the case. But, we have tied the evidence of our salvation and transformation to us becoming wealthy, which is where the problem lies. If we truthfully look at what God is teaching us, we will see that joy, peace, and true happiness do not come from the things we own. God teaches us that working to become rich will cause us more problems that anything else. In Ecclesiastes, we read that true happiness does not come from working so hard to become rich. (Ecclesiastes 5:10–17)

True happiness comes from God, and we receive it by seeking, worshipping, praising, and serving God not by serving our own agenda.

> *- Job 8:5–7 (NLT)—"But if you pray to God and seek the favor of the Almighty, and if you are pure and live with integrity, he will surely rise up and restore your happy home. And though you started with little, you will end with much."*

Receiving salvation: The true outcome that comes from being transformed is being confident in receiving salvation. Salvation is what God is holding to provide to those who trust in Him. It is the inheritance that is being kept in heaven for us. God is protecting us so we can receive this salvation that will be revealed on the last day.

> *- 1 Peter 1:3–5 (NLT)—"All praise to God, the Father of our Lord Jesus Christ. It is by his great mercy that we have been born again, because God raised Jesus Christ from the dead. Now we live with great expectation, and we have a priceless inheritance— an inheritance that is kept in heaven for you, pure and undefiled, beyond the reach of change and decay. And through your faith, God is protecting you by his power until you receive this salvation, which is ready to be revealed on the last day for all to see."*

Receiving joy and peace is an outcome of walking with God the Father and our Lord Jesus Christ. We should work to maintain our "completed" transformed state and not allow this world and the cares of this world to transform us back into the likeness of our human nature. For us to experience joy and peace, we have to be confident that our soul is protected in the loving arms of God. We have to guard against defiling our soul by giving God all control, so it is kept safe. A part of receiving joy and peace is having a clear understanding of how we can be truly happy, which comes from God. Anything else would give us a false sense of happiness that will fade away. Knowing that God is storing up an inheritance for those who trust in Him should give us joy and peace in this life. The results of being transformed into the likeness of Christ Jesus, is our salvation that comes from God; which produces the love of God in us.

The Fulfillment of our Purpose on Earth: Another outcome that comes from being transformed is fulfilling our purpose here on Earth. From the beginning, God created a plan for you and I to achieve His purpose. When we turned our hearts to the Father, He placed His Spirit in us to accomplish His plan. God causes everything to work together because He knew us in advance and chose us to be His sons and daughters through Jesus Christ. We come into right standing with God by doing His will and giving God all the glory. (Romans 8:27–30)

Once we are a part of Christ Jesus' body, we are called into service. We are assigned a good work to complete, for it is our earthly assignment from God. Learning God's purpose, His ways, and doing good, is the purpose for which you and I were created. We are called to produce for the kingdom of God. As we learn to walk in the light, we will be like a lampstand that cannot be hidden or put out.

> *- Matthew 5:16 (NKJV)—"Let your light so shine before men, that they may see your good works and glorify your Father in heaven."*

Completing your earthly assignment: When I look at the lives of those who accepted their calling from God, what becomes obvious, is that God allowed them to complete their earthly assignment. If you look at the lives of Abraham, Moses, David, Elijah, Peter, John, Paul, and our Lord Jesus Christ, just to name a few, they were allowed to complete the work God called them to do. This does not mean that they died in a way they would have preferred. It means they understood that their work was complete. It gave them a sense of joy, peace, and assurance that God was calling them to be with Him. There was no fear of death because Jesus Christ defeated death. There was no sorrow in their hearts because they knew where they were going. They felt only sadness because of those being left behind, but they rejoiced because God provided a way for all to come to Him. You can especially see this as Paul is completing his assignment on earth and he begins to struggle with being here on earth. He starts desiring to be with Christ more than continuing here on earth, but he understood the need to complete the full race.

- Philippians 1:21–24 (NLT)—"For to me, living means living for Christ, and dying is even better. But if I live, I can do more fruitful work for Christ. So I really don't know which is better. I'm torn between two desires: I long to go and be with Christ, which would be far better for me. But for your sakes, it is better that I continue to live."

When we are fully transformed, this should be our frame of reference. We will know when our assignment is complete and when it's time for us to go and be with Christ; which is better by far. There will be no more crying, no more suffering, no more selfishness, no more hurting one another, no more working to get rich, and no more sin.

- Revelation 21:4 (KJV)—"And God shall wipe away all tears from their eyes; and there shall be no more death, neither sorrow, nor crying, neither shall there be any more pain: for the former things are passed away."

Heavenly Rewards: In a world built on receiving results quickly and being able to see the fruit of their labor immediately, the reward system God offers is totally opposite. God knows we need to experience His love for us to have confirmation that we are accepted as His children. God implemented a big change from the first covenant to the second covenant. The first covenant, God put into place was a means for us to receive our rewards as we continue to move into His will. He provided great land and riches and had temples built so man could worship and praise Him. As He moved man from place to place, He decided when man was to take the plunder and when He wanted them to leave it. He decided who could join Israel, and who they needed to reject. He assigned leaders for His people and granted them great wealth while living on this earth. The reward system was immediate, much like what we desire today. In the second covenant, God decided, based on the way we managed wealth in the first convent, that He would not manifest His reward to us on earth as in times past. He continued to grant us His love, grace, and mercy and provide a means for us to experience joy and peace. But, for whatever reason, God's second convent is not based on us storing up earthly riches and land as in the past. I believe this occurred to keep us from making the same mistakes again, causing God to abandon His people for another 400 years. Jesus, in Matthew, teaches us that we must suffer as he did in order for us enter into God's Kingdom. He states that we should be glad to suffer on earth so our reward will be great in heaven.

> *- Matthew 5:11–12 (NLT)—"God blesses you when people mock you and persecute you and lie about you and say all sorts of evil things against you because you are my followers. Be happy about it! Be very glad! For a great reward awaits you in heaven."*

Jesus then teaches us to not allow our good deeds to be known on earth so we won't lose them in heaven.

> *- Matthew 6:1 (NLT)—"Watch out! Don't do your good deeds publicly, to be admired by others, for you will lose the reward from your Father in heaven."*

He goes on to teach us not to celebrate our giving in public, but to do our giving in private, where only God knows. That way, we can be rewarded by God and not man.

> *- Matthew 6:2–4 (NLT)—"When you give to someone in need, don't do as the hypocrites do—blowing trumpets in the synagogues and streets to call attention to their acts of charity! I tell you the truth, they have received all the reward they will ever get. But when you give to someone in need, don't let your left hand know what your right hand is doing. Give your gifts in private, and your Father, who sees everything, will reward you."*

What types of reward should we be expecting to receive from God? God will reward us with Salvation (Ephesians 2:9), and an inheritance (Colossians 3:24), He will allow us to eat from the fruit of life (Revelation 22:14), we will have heavenly manna to eat (Revelation 2:17), we will be given authority (Revelation 2:26), we will receive the morning star (Revelation

2:28), we will be given white robes to walk with Christ (Revelation 3:4), we will have protection (Revelation 3:10), we will be given a crown (Revelation 3:11), we will become citizens in the city of God (Revelation 3:12), and we will sit with Christ on his throne in victory (Revelation 3:21).

We need to buy gold from Christ that can never fade away by serving God and storing up our reward.

> - *Revelation 3:18 (NLT)—"So I advise you to buy gold from me— gold that has been purified by fire. Then you will be rich."*

We have to come to the point where nothing on this earth is worth more than what God has planned for us to receive. For all our suffering on this earth for Christ will not go unrewarded. We have the promises of God that there will be no more suffering, and no more crying. We need to seek first the Kingdom of God and all other things will be given to us so we can make it through.

> - *Matthew 6:31–34 (NLT)—"So don't worry about these things, saying, 'What will we eat? What will we drink? What will we wear?' These things dominate the thoughts of unbelievers, but your heavenly Father already knows all your needs. Seek the Kingdom of God above all else, and live righteously, and he will give you everything you need. So don't worry about tomorrow, for tomorrow will bring its own worries. Today's trouble is enough for today."*

How do we build up our reward? In the world today, the building of wealth comes from working our way up the corporate ladder, creating a business, developing worldly knowledge, developing our abilities, or storing up possessions so we can demonstrate to others how wise, successful, and smart we can be. Building up our wealth and reward in God, comes from us changing from within. God teaches us that, even though we may look successful in Christ from the outside, we can be a filthy rag on the inside. God will not be looking at our outward appearance or our accumulation of wealth as evidence that we have been transformed. He will be looking at what we have produced for His Kingdom and if we have cared for those He identified in His Word. I do have to say, He did not identify caring for a pastor and their family as those who need the help. Again, not to say we should not support a pastor's living, but God is focused on us helping the widows, the poor, the homeless, and leading the lost to Christ as part of building up our reward in heaven. Yes, as with any person who works in God's kingdom, a worker is worth his wages. But don't be confused that the latter work is better than the first. God has and always will care for His leaders; but, we are assigned the task of taking care of and encouraging the lost and bringing them to Christ. This work builds up a reward for us in Heaven.

> - Matthew 19:20–22 (NKJV)—"The young man said to Him, 'All these things I have kept from my youth. What do I still lack?' Jesus said to him, 'If you want to be perfect, go, sell what you have and give to the poor, and you will have treasure in heaven; and come, follow Me.' But when the young man heard that saying, he went away sorrowful, for he had great possessions."

Another part of building up our reward in heaven is the building up of our faith and seeking God in everything we do. God promises to reward us when we seek His will in our life.

> - Hebrews 11:6 (NLT)—"And it is impossible to please God without faith. Anyone who wants to come to him must believe that God exists and that he rewards those who sincerely seek him."

As we continue to grow in Christ Jesus, we begin building up our reward in heaven by doing good works for others. This is not to say we will not be blessed while we are on earth, but we are not trying to receive all that God has for us in a dying world. What will be our reward in heaven if we receive all of our rewards on earth? Do we think God will pay us multiple times for a good deed? (Luke 6:38 (NLT)

We must be careful not to think that, just by giving, God is going to store up a reward for us. First, we must believe in the reason God wants us to give, which is for all things to be made equal among believers.

> *- 2 Corinthians 8:11–14 (NLT)*—"Let the eagerness you showed in the beginning be matched now by your giving. Give in proportion to what you have. Whatever you give is acceptable if you give it eagerly. And give according to what you have, not what you don't have. Of course, I don't mean your giving should make life easy for others and hard for yourselves. I only mean that there should be some equality. Right now you have plenty and can help those who are in need. Later, they will have plenty and can share with you when you need it. In this way, things will be equal."

We must understand that giving is not in itself a means to enter into the kingdom of God.

> *- Jeremiah 17:9–10 (NLT)*—"The human heart is the most deceitful of all things, and desperately wicked. Who really knows how bad it is? But I, the Lord, search all hearts and examine secret motives. I give all people their due rewards, according to what their actions deserve."

We need to ask ourselves, what is the reason for our giving? Let's give in a way that God counts it toward our work of service to Him.

The last point I want to share about building up our reward in heaven, is regarding trusting in God. If we truly trust in God the Father and our Lord Jesus Christ, God is faithful and just to give us a reward. And the only way we learn to trust in God is by learning to be truly in love with God. And the only way we can come to love God is by learning from Him. And the only way we come to learn from God is by accepting His son. And the only way we come to accept Jesus Christ is by confessing, repenting, and believing.

> *- 1 Peter 1:8–9 (NLT)*—"You love him even though you have never seen him. Though you do not see him now, you trust him; and you rejoice with a glorious, inexpressible joy. The reward for trusting him will be the salvation of your souls."

Spiritual Transformation

Spiritual Body and Eternal Life: The final step in being transformed is for us to receive a spiritual body. God's goal is for us to inherit eternal life by passing through final judgment. Jesus Christ has been given the task of conducting the final judgment.

- *Matthew 25:31–46 (NLT)*—"But when the Son of Man comes in his glory, and all the angels with him, then he will sit upon his glorious throne. All the nations will be gathered in his presence, and he will separate the people as a shepherd separates the sheep from the goats. He will place the sheep at his right hand and the goats at his left. Then the King will say to those on his right, 'Come, you who are blessed by my Father, inherit the Kingdom prepared for you from the creation of the world. For I was hungry, and you fed me. I was thirsty, and you gave me a drink. I was a stranger, and you invited me into your home. I was naked, and you gave me clothing. I was sick, and you cared for me. I was in prison, and you visited me.' Then these righteous ones will reply, 'Lord, when did we ever see you hungry and feed you? Or thirsty and give you something to drink? Or a stranger and show you hospitality? Or naked and give you clothing? When did we ever see you sick or in prison and visit you?' And the King will say, 'I tell you the truth, when you did it to one of the least of these my brothers and sisters, you were doing it to me!' Then the King will turn to those on the left and say, 'Away with you, you cursed ones, into the eternal fire prepared for the devil and his demons. For I was hungry, and you didn't feed me. I was thirsty, and you didn't give me a drink. I was a stranger, and you didn't invite me into your home. I was naked, and you didn't give me clothing. I was sick and in prison, and you didn't visit me.' Then they will reply, 'Lord, when did we ever see you hungry or thirsty or a stranger or naked or sick or in prison, and not help you?' And he will answer, 'I tell you the truth, when you refused to help the least of these my brothers and sisters, you were refusing to help me.' And they will go away into eternal punishment, but the righteous will go into eternal life."

Passing through judgment is the key to receiving eternal life and a spiritual body; this is the final test. We can spend our life thinking there is no God or that we will have died by the time this occurs, but we must understand that believers and nonbelievers will be judged by Christ.

> *- 2 Corinthians 5:10 (NLT)—"For we must all stand before Christ to be judged. We will each receive whatever we deserve for the good or evil we have done in this earthly body." Therefore, there is no real discussion to this point, for the Word of God is true.*

Receiving eternal life: It's very important that we come to the understanding that there can only be two final states of our soul. Our soul will be condemned to eternal punishment, or we will be granted eternal life with Christ.

> *- Matthew 25:46 (KJV)—"And these shall go away into everlasting punishment: but the righteous into life eternal."*

While all of our bodies will die, what will happen to our souls is the question? Some may not even believe in our souls living beyond the life of our bodies, but whether they believe or not, killing the body does not kill our soul.

> *- Matthew 10:28 (NLT)—"Don't be afraid of those who want to kill your body; they cannot touch your soul. Fear only God, who can destroy both soul and body in hell."*

Why do we want to have eternal life with Christ? I would share with you that, from the beginning, God had a plan for a place called Eden, where He supplied all of man's needs. It was truly a beautiful place because God supplied everything. There was no poverty, sickness, or aging. All things lived from the source of life that came from God. We have not experienced this lifestyle yet, and the world we now live in doesn't even compare to the riches that God has for us who are changed and transformed in His image.

> *- Revelation 21:21–27 (NLT)—"The twelve gates were made of pearls—each gate from a single pearl! And the main street was pure gold, as clear as glass. I saw no temple in the city, for the Lord God Almighty and the Lamb are its temple. And the city has no need of sun or moon, for the glory of God illuminates the city,*

and the Lamb is its light. The nations will walk in its light, and the kings of the world will enter the city in all their glory. Its gates will never be closed at the end of day because there is no night there. And all the nations will bring their glory and honor into the city. Nothing evil will be allowed to enter, nor anyone who practices shameful idolatry and dishonesty—but only those whose names are written in the Lamb's Book of Life."

I hope and pray that you can see the need to be changed into a person that comes through the final judgment and receives eternal life.

Receiving a spiritual body: Because our spirit will be separated from our earthly body, there is a need for our spirit to have a body to live in. God created our current spirit to be housed in our human body; this was based on the first man, Adam. The prize
for overcoming this world and being delivered from this world is receiving a body from the spiritual man, Christ.

> *- 1 Corinthians 15:44 (KJV)—"It is sown a natural body; it is raised a spiritual body."*

In this way, we are made in his image.

> *- 1 Corinthians 15:44–49 (NIV)—"If there is a natural body, there is also a spiritual body. So it is written: 'The first man Adam became a living being;' the last Adam, a life-giving spirit. The spiritual did not come first, but the natural, and after that the spiritual. The first man was of the dust of the earth, the second man from heaven. As was the earthly man, so are those who are of the earth; and as is the man from heaven, so also are those who are of heaven. And just as we have borne the likeness of the earthly man, so shall we bear the likeness of the man from heaven."*

I believe one of the benefits of us receiving a spiritual body is that we will no longer be constrained by the dynamics of an earthly body. Our earthly bodies have to conform and are constrained by this world, but a spiritual body is constrained by the realm of heaven.

Spiritual Transformation

When we accept God the Father through our Lord Jesus Christ, we are saved and brought into right standing with God. We then have to allow God's Holy Spirit to cleanse us and get our mind, body, and soul, focused on the things of God and not ourselves. This also includes our thoughts, desires, and pleasures. It's important that we move forward in Christ to give God all the glory and not allow the cares of this world to entangle us back into worldly thinking, where Satan can once again control our soul. We must believe that to live for Christ is to die for Christ; anything short of total transformation and change will cause us to fool ourselves. We don't want to get to the throne of Christ and hear the words, "I don't know you." Instead, we want to hear the words, "Well done good and faithful servant." Spiritual transformation is not about what you and I think, it is about God's plan and His purpose for our lives. We cannot be caught sleeping or get tired of waiting and turn back. God knows the time and the season; that is why He is granting us more and more grace to allow us to overcome the greater sin that comes into the world, for times will get worse as Judgment Day approaches.

-Romans 5:20–21 (NLT)—"*God's law was given so that all people could see how sinful they were. But as people sinned more and more, God's wonderful grace became more abundant. So just as sin ruled over all people and brought them to death, now God's wonderful grace rules instead, giving us right standing with God and resulting in eternal life through Jesus Christ our Lord.*"

But we are not to use grace to cover up sin; we must use grace to help us complete the spiritual transformation. We need to let the Spirit of God rule in our hearts, mind, and body so we, the servants and children of God, can give all the glory to God the Father and our Lord Jesus Christ. Amen!

Prayer of Change and Transformation

Father God, in the name of your Son Jesus Christ our Savior, we ask that you receive us today and forgive us.
-We pray that all that comes from you is received by us for our salvation.
-We pray that your loving grace continues to cover us as we continue to allow your Holy Spirit to change our mind, to change our hearts, to change our bodies, into the glorious image of your Christ.
-We pray, Lord, that all who come to read this teaching be moved to call on your name with a sincere heart and spirit.
-We look forward to you moving us from a preparation stage into service for you.
-We look forward to you removing everything that is in us that is not pleasing to you.
-We look forward to you revealing the sin in us as we accept your truths.
-We look forward to the time when all sin is dead in our lives and you are glorified.
God, we pray that our transformation be used to draw others.
- As we are transformed, we seek harmony in the Body of Christ.
- As we are changed, we seek joy and peace in a dying world.
- As we grow, we look to magnify your name and will.
- Let thou will be done in all the Earth.
- Let every soul that is lost be found crying out to you.
- Let those who are confused be found seeking your face.
- Let those who are self-righteous find freedom in your will and purpose.
- Let those who are prideful be found humble in your sight.
- Let us all be transformed into the likeness of your blessed Son.
- Let the whole world cry out the name of Christ Jesus.
All to the glory of God the Father. Amen.

Spiritual Transformation

A New Creation

The purpose of the following chart is to provide a visual understanding of the content in this chapter. The reader can use this chart to help seek a deeper understanding into the meaning of transformation as described in the Bible. We all must experience transformation; it's just a matter of what type of transformation are we going through, religious or spiritual? Many of us have gone through the process of accepting our Lord Jesus Christ. After we are connected to Jesus Christ, the question is, how are we being transformed or do we see the need to change and become a new creation?

We are not looking to become the modern day Pharisees or Sadducees; we are open to the Holy Spirit and our Lord Jesus Christ cutting away our sinful nature. Once we have become free, through the blood of Christ and the teaching of the Holy Spirit, we do not turn back and start defiling our new creation. We cannot desire to continue in our sinful nature, making the blood of Jesus Christ and the teaching of God ineffective in our lives. We cannot deny or reject the calling and purpose of God for our lives. We are now the children of the Most High God, and we are obedient in every way.

A New Creation
Through Transformation

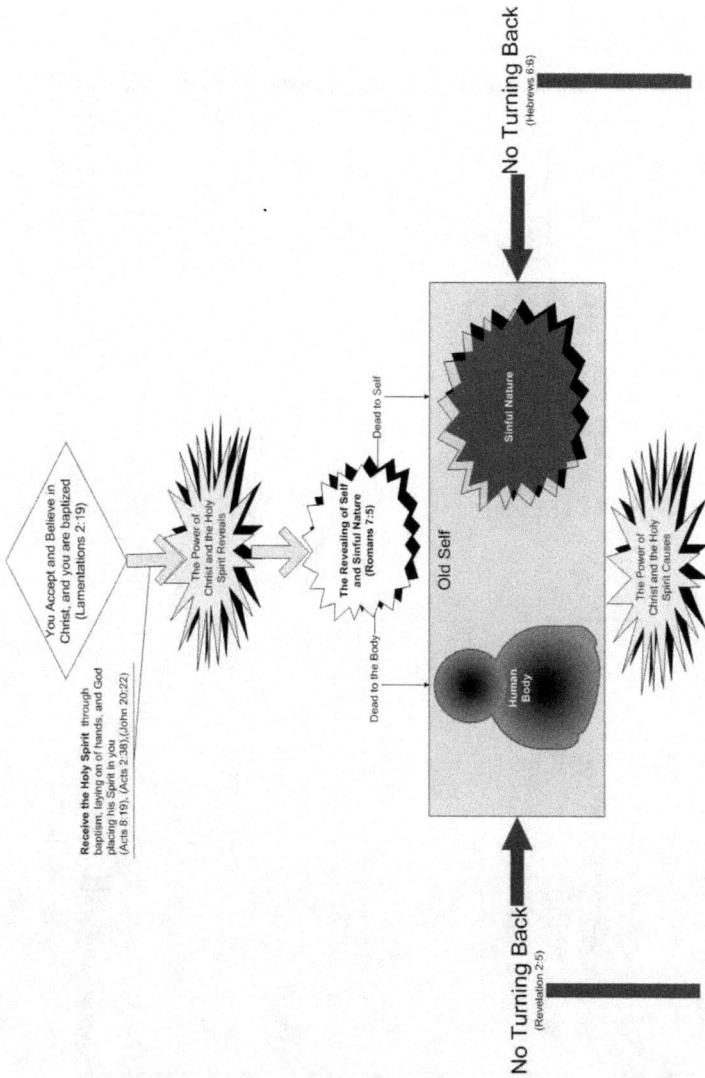

You Accept and Believe in Christ, and you are baptized (Lamentations 2:19)

Receive the Holy Spirit through baptism, laying on of hands, and God placing his Spirit in you (Acts 8 19), (Acts 2:38),(John 20:22)

The Power of Christ and the Holy Spirit Reveals

The Revealing of Self and Sinful Nature (Romans 7:5)

Dead to Self

Dead to the Body

Sinful Nature

Old Self

Human Body

The Power of Christ and the Holy Spirit Causes

No Turning Back
(Hebrews 6:6)

No Turning Back
(Revelation 2:5)

Spiritual Transformation

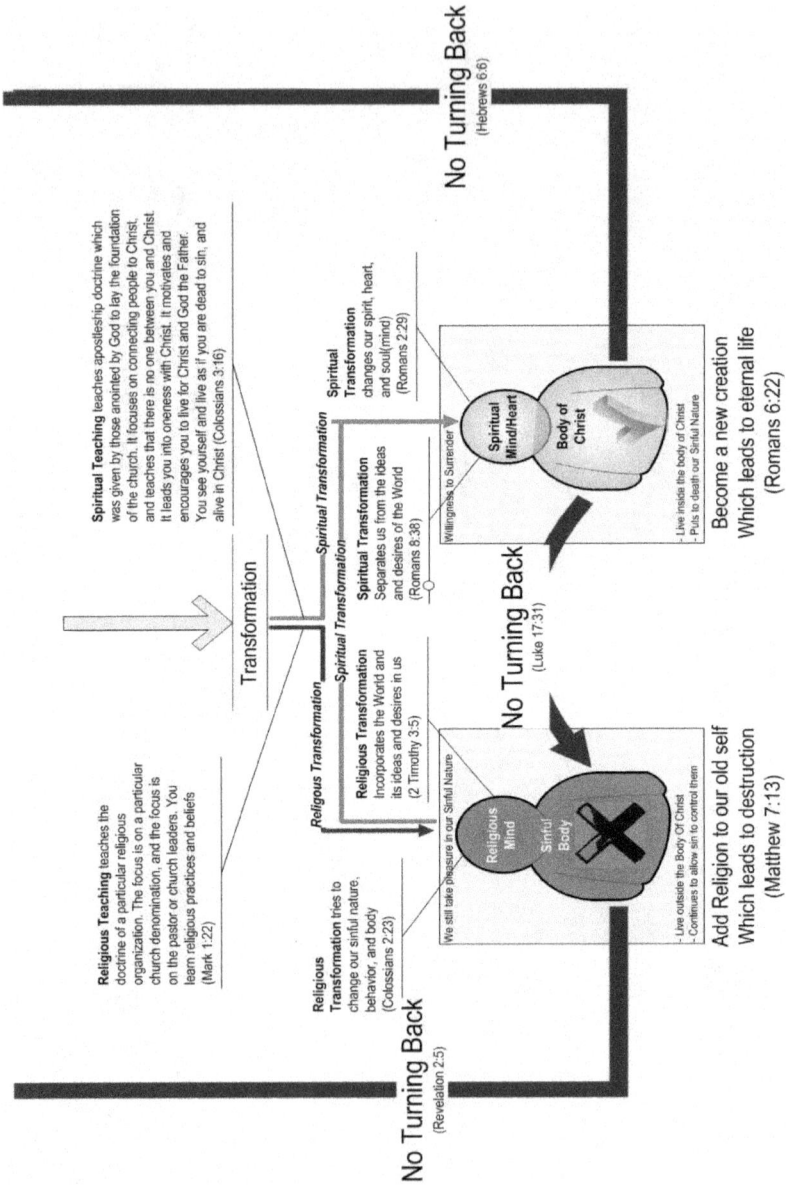

Religious Teaching teaches the doctrine of a particular religious organization. The focus is on a particular church denomination, and the focus is on the pastor or church leaders. You learn religious practices and beliefs (Mark 1:22)

Spiritual Teaching teaches apostleship doctrine which was given by those anointed by God to lay the foundation of the church. It focuses on connecting people to Christ, and teaches that there is no one between you and Christ. It leads you into oneness with Christ. It motivates and encourages you to live for Christ and God the Father. You see yourself and live as if you are dead to sin, and alive in Christ (Colossians 3:16)

Transformation

Religious Transformation

Spiritual Transformation

Spiritual Transformation

Religious Transformation tries to change our sinful nature, behavior, and body (Colossians 2:23)

Religious Transformation Incorporates the World and its ideas and desires in us (2 Timothy 3:5)

Spiritual Transformation Separates us from the ideas and desires of the World (Romans 8:38)

Spiritual Transformation changes our spirit, heart, and soul(mind) (Romans 2:29)

Willingness to Surrender

Spiritual Mind/Heart

Body of Christ

Religious Mind

Sinful Body

We still take pleasure in our Sinful Nature

- Live outside the Body Of Christ
- Continues to allow sin to control them

- Live inside the body of Christ
- Puts to death our Sinful Nature

No Turning Back
(Luke 17:31)

No Turning Back
(Revelation 2:5)

No Turning Back
(Hebrews 6:6)

Add Religion to our old self Which leads to destruction
(Matthew 7:13)

Become a new creation Which leads to eternal life
(Romans 6:22)

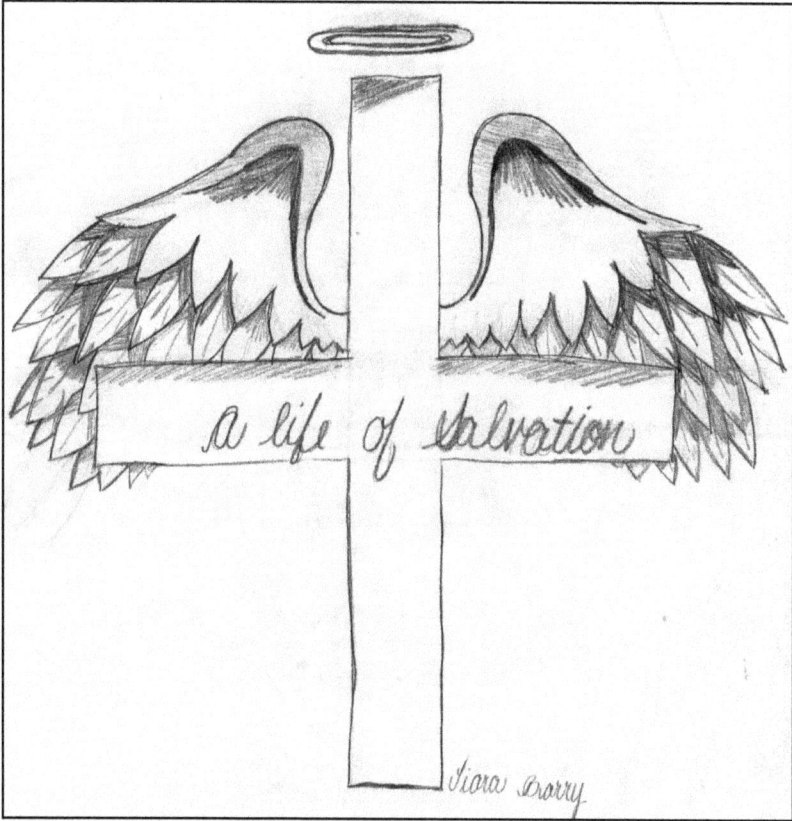

A Life of Salvation

Chapter 5

THE WORD of GOD IS LIKE

By Donna Maria Barry

The WORD of GOD is very much like
A LIGHT which brightens our pathway
God's word is a lamp unto our feet
From his guidance we must not stray

THE WORD of GOD is very much like
A WEAPON against Satan our foe
Causing him threat he will run in defeat
While in the knowledge of God we grow

THE WORD of GOD is very much like
A MAKEOVER transforming our attitude
Becoming his likeness both inside and out
While representing him with gratitude

THE WORD of GOD is very much like
A SCALE used for measurement
Do we measure up to the standards of God
Or lack integrity and need to repent

THE WORD of GOD is very much like
A COAT of WAX as our protection
Constantly repelling the world's point of view
And allowing them to see God's reflection

THE WORD of GOD is our Standard for Life
The most exceptional form of learning
By practicing it with a committed heart
Through faithfulness we'll develop a yearning

A Life of Salvation

There are many different teachings going on in the world today about how we obtain salvation. Some believe, the only thing we have to do is confess and believe in Jesus Christ. Others believe, we have to continue seeking God's grace and mercy until the end to be saved. There are others who believe. we cannot lose our salvation. And still others who believe, we don't need Jesus; we can just go to God directly. We will travel through the Bible to understand what God wants us to believe regarding seeking salvation. One of the first questions we will cover is "what is salvation?" We will cover the following points to give us a clear picture.

- What is salvation, and why do we need it?
- How do we receive salvation?
- Can we lose our salvation?
- What about believers who continue in rebellion
- How do we live a life of salvation?

What Is Salvation, and Why Do We Need It?

We are all born under sin from the time Adam and Eve refused God's plan of salvation by breaking the rules; we all have been cursed. Salvation is our ability to regain the relationship that we had with God at the start of the creation of the earth. In the Old Testament, God would use prophets and priests to guide and bring people into His presence. God even came to earth to show Himself to us in a cloud.

> *- Jeremiah 26:4–5 (NIV)—"Say to them, 'This is what the Lord says: If you do not listen to me and follow my law, which I have set before you, and if you do not listen to the words of my servants the prophets, whom I have sent to you again and again (though you have not listened) ... .'"*

His purpose was and is to bless those who believe in His power and authority as their creator. As we know from the Old Testament, God worked with us so many times, teaching us His rules and forgiving us when we sinned. God worked with our religious leaders (prophets and priests), trying to keep us on track until the coming of His son. We failed the test, and

God withdrew himself from our presence because of our sinful ways.

- Malachi 2:7–9 (NLT)—"The words of a priest's lips should preserve knowledge of God, and people should go to him for instruction, for the priest is the messenger of the Lord of Heaven's Armies. But you priests have left God's paths. Your instructions have caused many to stumble into sin. 'You have corrupted the covenant I made with the Levites,' says the Lord of Heaven's Armies. 'So I have made you despised and humiliated in the eyes of all the people. For you have not obeyed me but have shown favoritism in the way you carry out my instructions.'"

Because God is such a loving God, He never forgot about us. He prepared His son for reconciling us to Himself through the blood offering that He required from the creation of the world. He created a new convent that could not be broken based on man's sin and misdeeds. As we review the following scriptures, Jesus Christ, the Son of God, has been given all power and authority to execute God the Father's will to save those who are lost. In Matthew, we learn how Jesus Christ came into the world and that his purpose is to save God's people from their sins.

- Matthew 1:21 (NLT)—"And she will have a son, and you are to name him Jesus, for he will save his people from their sins."

Also in Matthew, John the Baptist hesitated to baptize Jesus Christ because he knew who Jesus was, but Jesus Christ insisted that the will of God the Father must be done. We go on to learn that John agreed, and, through the baptism process, Jesus Christ received God's Holy Spirit. Then, God the Father, speaking from Heaven, confirmed to those who were witnessing this event, that Jesus Christ is indeed the Son of God. Jesus Christ taught his disciplines that he has been given all authority in heaven and on earth. He sent them out under his authority to baptize them in the name of the Father, Son, and Holy Spirit. The disciples had to teach those who were baptized to obey all the commands of Christ. Based on our obedience, Christ promises he will always be with us all the way until the end of the world. In Luke, we see where Jesus was visiting the A Life of Salvation homes of those in the community and observed the way they lived to determine if they were demonstrating the principles of God in their lives. Jesus Christ states again that his purpose is to seek and save those who are lost.

- Luke 19:9–10 (NLT)—"Jesus responded, 'Salvation has come to this home today, for this man has shown himself to be a true son of Abraham. For the Son of Man came to seek and save those who are lost.'"

In John, he shares the teaching of God's love for us and the sacrifice of His one and only Son so we will not perish but have eternal life. We also learn that the first coming of Christ to earth was not to judge the world but to save us through his blood. John teaches us that Jesus Christ is the gate for his sheep and anyone who came before Christ was a thief and a robber. We must learn to listen to the voice of Christ and not listen to those who came to deceive us. When we accept Jesus Christ, we will be able to come and go freely and find good pastures.

- John 3:16–17 (NLT)—"For God loved the world so much that he gave his one and only Son, so that everyone who believes in him will not perish but have eternal life. God sent his Son into the world not to judge the world, but to save the world through him."

Jesus Christ's purpose is to give us a rich and satisfying life through him. When we call on the name of the Lord, we will be saved. We have to understand that we all have sinned and fall short of the glory of God, so we need to come through Jesus Christ to receive salvation.

- Acts 2:21 (NLT)—"But everyone who calls on the name of the Lord will be saved."

Jesus Christ came to save us from ourselves and Satan's grasp. Through baptism, we are born again into a new creation. We need to (not should) see ourselves dead to the ways of the world and alive to the will of Jesus Christ and God the Father. Now that God has granted us a new body through the blood of Jesus, we are free to approach God the Father in the name of

Jesus Christ to develop a relationship through faith and trust with God and our Lord Jesus Christ. This is the Good News that Jesus brought to share with us. We can now depend on God's grace and mercy to sustain us as we continue to develop a deeper relationship with Him. Now, accepting Christ as our Lord and Savior gets us in the front door. Salvation is a process of being saved not only from the sins we committed before we knew Christ, but also from all our transgressions after we have come to know him. The process that Jesus Christ went through to make a way for us to be received by the Father was a big deal. In Colossians, we see that Jesus Christ performed a spiritual circumcision on us to cut away our sinful nature so we can be received. We were buried with Christ when we were baptized, and, through this baptism, we were raised in Christ. We are now a part of the Body of Christ and should live our lives based on who we now are in Christ, not on who we were in the world.

> - *Colossians 2:11–12 (NLT)—"When you came to Christ, you were 'circumcised,' but not by a physical procedure. Christ performed a spiritual circumcision—the cutting away of your sinful nature. For you were buried with Christ when you were baptized. And with him you were raised to new life because you trusted the mighty power of God, who raised Christ from the dead."*

And since we have been made right with God the Father through the blood of Christ, we have been saved from the punishment or condemnation of our sins. Through the sacrifice process that Christ went through for us, our relationship and friendship with God the Father has been restored. Christ was obedient to the calling of the Father, even while we were still enemies of God. In this way, all who accept, believe, and trust in our Lord Jesus Christ can be saved through his blood. Because of Christ's great love for us and his obedience to the will of God the Father, we can rejoice in our wonderful new relationship with God the Father because Jesus Christ our Lord has made us friends of God.

> - *Romans 5:9–10 (NLT)—"And since we have been made right in God's sight by the blood of Christ, he will certainly save us from God's condemnation. For since our friendship with God was restored by the death of his Son while we were still his enemies, we will certainly be saved through the life of his Son."*

A Life of Salvation

Those who have not accepted Jesus Christ as their Lord and Savior, are still under the rules of the old covenant (the law); therefore, they cannot enter into a relationship with God because He rejected the sacrifices of the Old Testament because of our great and many sins. The old covenant could not save us because of the weakness of our sinful nature. As mentioned earlier, Christ came to cut away our sinful nature so we can be received by God the Father. In the Body of Christ, there is an end to allowing sin to have control over us. When Christ completed the sacrifice process, it allowed the fulfillment of the law to be completed in a way that brought full satisfaction to God the Father. It allowed us to no longer follow our sinful nature but instead to follow the Spirit of God. In 2 Corinthians, we come to understand that our life is a Christ-like fragrance that rises up to God the Father. While we all give off a fragrance that God can smell, the fragrance from those who are being saved is different from those who are perishing. There is a dreadful smell of death coming from those who are doomed. But we who are being saved have a fragrance like that of a life-giving perfume to God the Father.

- 2 Corinthians 2:15–16 (NLT)—"Our lives are a Christ-like fragrance rising up to God. But this fragrance is perceived differently by those who are being saved and by those who are perishing. To those who are perishing, we are a dreadful smell of death and doom. But to those who are being saved, we are a life-giving perfume. And who is adequate for such a task as this?"

Now that we understand what salvation is and why we need it, let's talk a little bit about the promises that come with salvation. God promises that, once we accept Jesus Christ as our Lord and Savior and are baptized, we are given his Holy Spirit to reside inside of us as a guarantee of His promises. We also understand that receiving God's Holy Spirit is a gift. There is nothing we can do to earn it. There is no price we can pay for it, and there is no work you can do it receive it. It is a gift to those who believe and do God's will. Included in God's promises is the granting of eternal life if we continue to grow, overcome, and endure until the end. We also know that Jesus Christ is working to intercede for us because of his great love. When we trust in God, He will reveal his truth to us. Another aspect of God's promises is that, if we died with Christ, we will also be resurrected with him when he returns. Let's review a few scriptures to confirm these points. In Ephesians, we learn that, through believing in the Good News, we get confirmation that God is working to save us. When we place our beliefs, hopes, and desires in Christ, he identifies us as one of his own and gives us the Holy Spirit. This fulfills a promise from God the Father long before you and I were born. The Spirit of God has been given to us as a guarantee of our inheritance that God promised to those who continue to seek Him. We have to remember that we were purchased for a very high price. The blood of Jesus Christ was very precious to God the Father, and there is nothing you and I have that equates to the price of one drop of the blood of Christ. The best we can do is to give our lives to Christ and continue to worship and praise him for making a way for us to be in a relationship with him and God the Father. We must not take this lightly and think we can continue as we are as we call on the name of our Lord Jesus Christ for help. God is so rich in mercy and He loves us so much that He gives us life through the raising of Christ from the dead. We must be willing to surrender ourselves to Christ in every way.

> - *Ephesians 1:13–14 (NLT)—"And now you Gentiles have also heard the truth, the Good News that God saves you. And when you believed in Christ, he identified you as his own by giving you the Holy Spirit, whom he promised long ago. The Spirit is God's guarantee that he will give us the inheritance he promised and that he has purchased us to be his own people. He did this so we would praise and glorify him."*

Again, there is no work you and I can do to receive grace and salvation from God the Father and our Lord Jesus Christ; it is given as part of God's plan of salvation for those whom He calls and those who surrender to Him. We are God's masterpiece that He created from clay. God is molding us into a new person in Christ Jesus so we can do good things based on His plan for us. Based on the sins each one of us HAVE committed, in His justice, God should have put us all to death, because that is what our lives deserve. But God chose to save us through our Lord Jesus Christ and not pour out His anger on us. We have confidence that, if we develop a true relationship with God the Father and our Lord Jesus Christ, which is not based on our needs, but on God's plan, then whether we are alive or dead when Christ returns, we will be with him forever. If we are true to the Spirit of God and allow God's Spirit to transform and change us into the likeness of Christ, we should be encouraged and build each other up, for God is more than able to deliver on His promises.

> *- Ephesians 2:8–10 (NLT)—"God saved you by his grace when you believed. And you can't take credit for this; it is a gift from God. Salvation is not a reward for the good things we have done, so none of us can boast about it. For we are God's masterpiece. He has created us anew in Christ Jesus, so we can do the good things he planned for us long ago."*

As we learn in 1 Timothy, when we work to understand the truth from God, it is good and pleasing to Him and our Lord Jesus Christ. We come to fully understand that there is only one God and one mediator who can reconcile God with humanity, and that man is Christ Jesus. He gave his life to purchase freedom for everyone so those who are in sin can be saved.

> *- 1 Timothy 2:3–6 (NLT)—"This is good and pleases God our Savior, who wants everyone to be saved and to understand the truth. For there is only one God and one Mediator who can reconcile God and humanity—the man Christ Jesus. He gave his life to purchase freedom for everyone. This is the message God gave to the world at just the right time."*

In 2 Timothy, we learn that God saved us and called us to live a holy life, not because we deserve it, but because this was God's plan before the beginning of time. God did this to show us His grace through Christ Jesus. Jesus Christ broke the power of death that kept us from God, and, when God raised him from the dead, his life illuminated a way for us to live and have immortality. Our Lord Jesus Christ paid the price to have all our sins washed away in order for us to be born again and be given a new life that glorifies God. Because Jesus lives forever, we will be raised with him in his glory. Today, we work to overcome and continue in Christ's grace and mercy as he intercedes on our behalf to God the Father. Christ has been given the highest place of honor, and those who believe in Christ will also so walk in his honor and glory, if we don't turn away.

> *- 2 Timothy 1:8–10 (NLT)—"For God saved us and called us to live a holy life. He did this, not because we deserved it, but because that was his plan from before the beginning of time—to show us his grace through Christ Jesus. And now he has made all of this plain to us by the appearing of Christ Jesus, our Savior. He broke the power of death and illuminated the way to life and immortality through the Good News."*

When we study God's Word, work to do His will, pray in the Spirit, and remain in Christ, we will continue to grow. As our relationship with Christ grows, he will reveal his kindness and love to us. Because we are now a part of the Body of Christ, he generously pours out His Spirit upon us. As we grow and mature in Christ, we begin to devote ourselves to the work we are called to do. Peter teaches us that, through Christ, we come to trust in God and we place our faith and hope in God because He raised Christ from the dead and gave him great glory. When Christ reveals his love to us, we must show sincere love to each other as brothers and sisters. We must learn to love each other deeply with all our heart and our new life will last forever because it comes from God. We also learn that Christ not only taught us while he was here on earth, but when he was crucified and died he went to those who had died long ago whose spirits were being held in prison so they too could have the opportunity to accept Jesus Christ as their Lord and Savior.

> *- 1 Peter 1:21–23 (NLT)—"Through Christ you have come to trust in God. And you have placed your faith and hope in God because he raised Christ from the dead and gave him great glory. You were cleansed from your sins when you obeyed the truth, so now you must show sincere love to each other as brothers and sisters. Love each other deeply with all your heart. For you have been born again, but not to a life that will quickly end. Your new life will last forever because it comes from the eternal, living word of God."*

Afterward, Christ departed and went up to heaven, where he is seated in the place of honor next to God the Father, with all the angels, authorities, and powers under his authority. We have full confidence that God the Father, through our Lord Jesus Christ; will come to gather us up unto himself. What a great day that will be.

> *- 1 Peter 3:18–22 (NLT)—"Christ suffered for our sins once for all time. He never sinned, but he died for sinners to bring you safely home to God. He suffered physical death, but he was raised to life in the Spirit. So he went and preached to the spirits in prison— those who disobeyed God long ago when God waited patiently while Noah was building his boat. Only eight people were saved from drowning in that terrible flood. And that water is a picture of baptism, which now saves you, not by removing dirt from your body, but as a response to God from a clean conscience. It is effective because of the resurrection of Jesus Christ. Now Christ has gone to heaven. He is seated in the place of honor next to God, and all the angels and authorities and powers accept his authority."*

How Do We Receive Salvation?

It is important to know that receiving salvation is not only based on us confessing that Jesus Christ is our Lord and Savior. We also have to repent from our sins and be baptized, which means we have to turn away from our sins and no longer commit them. There are a few things we receive with salvation—being accepted in the Kingdom of God, being born again, having our sins forgiven, and receiving God's Holy Spirit. We are a mixture of a lot of different people in the Body of Christ. We have an obligation to each other, as a part of one body, to encourage, suffer for, and sustain one another. We should help each other to walk in the presence of Jesus Christ. If one of us begins to wander off, we should work to bring this person back by showing and sharing with them the love of God, the patience of God, and the Word of God. We are still working to accomplish what John the Baptist started. We are still working to preach and teach others about the need to repent, for the kingdom of God is still at hand. God's plan is still being brought to a conclusion, so repent and live right while there is still time.

- Matthew 3:1–2 (NLT)—"In those days, John the Baptist came to the Judean wilderness and began preaching. His message was, 'Repent of your sins and turn to God, for the Kingdom of Heaven is near.'"

Through the teachings of John the Baptist, we see the outcome of trying to obtain our salvation through a religious process. The Pharisees and Sadducees practiced religion more that you and I could ever carry out today. But, John the Baptist severely warned them that carrying out religious traditions will not allow us to receive salvation. We come to understand that it takes believing, to receive salvation, and that requires us to have faith. But we know it's not just about saying we believe; we not only have to confess that we believe, we have to demonstrate in our hearts and through our actions that we truly believe. We learn in John that, unless we are born again, we cannot enter into the kingdom of God. We need to be saved from our sins and be born again (made into a new creation) to enter into the kingdom of God, which is the completion of our salvation.

- John 3:4–7 (NLT)—"'What do you mean?' exclaimed Nicodemus. 'How can an old man go back into his mother's womb and be born again?' Jesus replied, 'I assure you, no one can enter the Kingdom of God without being born of water and the Spirit. Humans can reproduce only human life, but the Holy Spirit gives birth to spiritual life. So don't be surprised when I say, "You must be born again."'"

This is pointed out to us by Peter in Acts when he shares the same message that John the Baptist shared, which is the requirement for us to repent and be baptized in the name of Jesus Christ, so there can be a remission of our sins and we can receive the Holy Spirit. Because we have been forgiven from our sins and we are a new creation in Christ, we don't consider the power of the cross foolish. Those who take the power of the cross foolishly are headed for destruction.

- Acts 2:38 (NLT)—"Peter replied, 'Each of you must repent of your sins, turn to God, and be baptized in the name of Jesus Christ to show that you have received forgiveness for your sins. Then you will receive the gift of the Holy Spirit.'"

Those who accept, live, and seek salvation, understand they are being saved by the power of God. We know that there is only one body, and we who are called by God and our Lord Jesus Christ must build up the body through our demonstration of Godly love and encouragement to believers and nonbelievers. We are made righteous in God's sight when we live by faith. As it is stated in Philippians, suffering for Christ is a privilege. The Bible teaches us that the body is made up of many parts, but all of the many parts make up the one whole body. Because of Christ's body, we are all made into one family, which is the family of God.

- 1 Corinthians 1:18 (NLT)—"The message of the cross is foolish to those who are headed for destruction! But we who are being saved know it is the very power of God."

Whether Jew or Gentiles, we were all accepted into the body of Christ when we were baptized by the one Spirit, and we share that same Spirit that guides us into salvation. Those who receive the teaching of God the Father and our Lord Jesus Christ receive that which comes from God. As we continue to grow, our receiving of salvation is made whole by the Holy Spirit. As we grow, we remain open-minded about the truth that comes from God, even if it requires us to change our thinking about ourselves and others. More important than carrying out religious practices, is our continued absorption of the truth that comes from God, which continues to transform and change us into the image of Christ Jesus.

- 1 Corinthians 12:12–13 (NLT)—"The human body has many parts, but the many parts make up one whole body. So it is with the body of Christ. Some of us are Jews, some are Gentiles, some are slaves, and some are free. But we have all been baptized into one body by one Spirit, and we all share the same Spirit."

A Life of Salvation

Can We Lose Our Salvation?

Now the question is, "Can we lose our salvation?" I, too, being brought up in a particular church doctrine, believed that I could not lose my salvation. After much study, prayer, and the Holy Spirit teaching me, I now understand God's truths based on his Word. Jesus spoke about us losing our salt in Mark

> - Mark 9:49–50 (NLT)—"For everyone will be tested with fire. Salt is good for seasoning. But if it loses its flavor, how do you make it salty again? You must have the qualities of salt among yourselves and live in peace with each other."
> Therefore, he lets us know that, if we lose our saltiness, we are not worth anything and we cannot be salted again.

In Ezekiel, we learn that, if we who have been brought into righteous standing with God turn from God, we will be forgotten and die in our sins. Jesus, in Matthew, teaches us that we need to endure until the end to be saved. Then, there is the parable in Luke where we can lose our salvation because we care more for this world than for God's will. Again, in Luke, we see that if we get tired of waiting on Christ to return and go back to committing sin, we will be placed with the unbelievers. We know that it is God who counts those who love and seek him as righteous. And as explained in Ezekiel, God will reward those he deems righteous with a reward, but those who are considered wicked will be punished for their wickedness. In these scriptures, God shares His thoughts and ways of justice by letting us know that, if the wicked turn from their sin, they will be forgiven. But if a righteous person starts to carry out sinful acts, their righteous acts will be forgotten and they will die in their sins. So God looks down on us to determine our state of being, and, based on what He sees, we are rewarded or condemned, all based on how we continue to conduct ourselves. (Ezekiel 18:20–24)

In Matthew, we are given a revelation of a future time, which is now our time. It describes the time in which sin is rampant everywhere, everyone will be chasing after money, and the love of many will grow cold. But, even as this is taking place, the Good News of God will continue to be preached throughout the whole world. This is all occurring as we approach the end of God's plan of salvation for the world.

> *- Matthew 24:10–14 (NLT)—"And many will turn away from me and betray and hate each other. And many false prophets will appear and will deceive many people. Sin will be rampant everywhere, and the love of many will grow cold. But the one who endures to the end will be saved. And the Good News about the Kingdom will be preached throughout the whole world, so that all nations will hear it; and then the end will come."*

We then take a look at a parable of Jesus Christ in Luke, we come to understand that the devil is present every time a person gives themselves to Christ. It states how the devil comes after the person who has heard the Word of God and he takes away the word from their heart, preventing them from believing and being saved. This is the first way salvation is prevented from growing is us. It goes on to speak of the Word of God falling on the rocky soil, which are those who hear the Word of God and receive it with joy, but only believe for a little while and temptation comes and they fall away. This is the second way salvation is lost after receiving the Word of God. The parable continues to explain how the Word of God falls on the thorns, which represent those who hear the Word of God, but the cares of this world and the desire to be rich choke out the Word of God from within them, so they never grow into maturity. This is the third way we lose our salvation. But, because Jesus Christ is always providing a way out of our troubles; He speaks of the Word of God that falls on the good soil, which represents those who are honest and good-hearted and cling to the Word of God and patiently produce a huge harvest for God. (Luke 8:11–15)

Jesus Christ continues to teach us in Luke about not losing our salvation by illustrating the work of farmer, stating that no one having put his hand to the plow and looking back is fit for the Kingdom of God. We cannot begin on the road to salvation that leads to eternal life and look back and desire the life we had before or even reach back to enjoy sinful pleasures that we conducted before and believe that we are still on the road to salvation. We have taken a detour, and this road leads to destruction.

> *- Luke 9:60–62 (NLT)—"But Jesus told him, 'Let the spiritually dead bury their own dead! Your duty is to go and preach about the Kingdom of God.' Another said, 'Yes, Lord, I will follow you, but first let me say good-bye to my family.' But Jesus told him, 'Anyone who puts a hand to the plow and then looks back is not fit for the Kingdom of God.'*

I just love to read and hear the teachings of Jesus Christ as he continues teaching Luke. In Luke, we learn that a good and sensible servant is one to whom the master gives the responsibility of managing his other household servants and feeding them. It would be nice if all those who are called to lead God's people would take this teaching to heart. Jesus Christ goes on to share with us that if the master returns and finds that the servant has done a good job, he will reward that servant for taking care of, managing, and feeding those who live in God's household. If that servant tries to outsmart his master or change the responsibilities he has been given, starts to mistreating those in God's household, and starts partying or getting drunk, then the master will return unannounced and unexpected and he will cut the servant into pieces and banish him with the unfaithful. This is another way we could lose our salvation.

> *- Luke 12:42–46 (NLT)—"And the Lord replied, 'A faithful, sensible servant is one to whom the master can give the responsibility of managing his other household servants and feeding them. If the master returns and finds that the servant has done a good job, there will be a reward. I tell you the truth, the master will put that servant in charge of all he owns. But what if the servant thinks, 'My master won't be back for a while,' and he begins beating the other servants, partying, and getting drunk? The master will return unannounced and unexpected, and he will cut the servant in pieces and banish him with the unfaithful."*

In Hebrews, we learn that, if we who have partaken of God's mercy and grace decide to no longer believe in God, we cannot obtain repentance from God again. These are very strong scriptures that should guide us into a lifetime of obedience to God and our Lord Jesus Christ. It is not just a matter for getting saved from past sins. But, we must endure and overcome to enter into God's kingdom and obtain the prize for our work, by having faith in Jesus Christ. While some of us may have experienced the presence of God in our life, this scripture is speaking to those who have walked with God the Father and our Lord Jesus Christ and they have been transformed and changed. God has poured into them His power and authority, and they have experienced a deep relationship with God the Father and our Lord Jesus Christ. The truth of God has been revealed to these individuals, and they have been led by the Holy Spirit. But, for whatever reason, they have decided to not just transgress against God, but they no longer believe in God's truth or the Word of God. When this happens, that person does not have the opportunity to obtain salvation again because it would be like nailing our Lord Jesus Christ to the cross all over again, and that is not a plan that God the Father will allow to happen.

> *- Hebrews 6:4–6 (NLT)—"For it is impossible to bring back to repentance those who were once enlightened—those who have experienced the good things of heaven and shared in the Holy Spirit, who have tasted the goodness of the word of God and the power of the age to come—and who then turn away from God. It is impossible to bring such people back to repentance; by rejecting the Son of God, they themselves are nailing him to the cross once again and holding him up to public shame."*

There is the possibility that some believers could wander away from Christ, but we who are believers should assist in bringing them back so they will be saved from death and again bring about the forgiveness of their sins. In the book of James, we learn of this teaching. Just like God the Father and our Lord Jesus Christ is hard at work teaching and saving us from destruction, we have to be willing to focus on helping others who wonder away because of circumstances and situations in life. We do not want to see them return back to a life that is filled with darkness and shame. God promises that he will never leave us and he will always provide a way out for those who continue to seek and place their hope and trust in God the

Father and our Lord Jesus Christ. While God is not walking around on earth with us, as He did in the times of Adam and Eve, He is very much present with us in Spirit. Jesus Christ has gone back to sit at the right hand of God and continues working until the judgment time. We still need to endure and relish the love that comes from above and the guarantee that was placed in us, God's Holy Spirit. Yes, we can choose to no longer listen to, follow, or receive the salvation that God has planned for each one of us. However, there will be severe consequences depending on the decision we make. If we continue to believe, we have the promises of God, which He holds in His hand for those who love Him and place their trust in His love for us. We are faced with a choice—whom will we serve each and every day? For this reason, we need to be renewed each day so we are reminded of God's Word and our responsibility to the throne of God.

> - *James 5:19–20 (NLT)—"My dear brothers and sisters, if someone among you wanders away from the truth and is brought back, you can be sure that whoever brings the sinner back will save that person from death and bring about the forgiveness of many sins."*

What about Believers Who Continue in Rebellion?

The granting of grace and mercy to believers did not start with the New Testament, though Jesus Christ fulfilled its purpose. In the Old Testament, we learn of God's ways that lead to a Holy life, as well as his grace for Israel and Judah. We learn that God required blood for the forgiveness of sin. The priests would go into the Holy Place in the temple to offer a sacrifice for themselves and for Israel's rebellious and sinful ways. God teaches us that, if we disobey his Word, His anger will completely destroy those who walk in disobedience. Even in the Old Testament, God showed those who loved him grace and mercy. In the book of Exodus, God warns us to pay close attention to Him and obey His instructions. God teaches us to not rebel against His angels who are sent to instruct us because they are God's representatives and He will not forgive our rebellion. God also lets us know that, if we do obey and follow all His instructions, then He will be an enemy to our enemies and oppose those who oppose us. Just as in the Old Testament, God created a process for our defiling sins and rebellious ways to be forgiven. In the Old Testament, it was through the blood of animals; but, that same sacrificing was accomplished through the blood of Jesus Christ. We must always remember that there are always two sides to God. Based on our heart and our motives, He will either provide the things He has promised to us or He will bring disaster on us for disobeying Him. (Exodus 23:20–22)

If we continue to rebel against the will of God, His anger will burn against us and the things God has provided will quickly vanish before us. Again, we are warned that, if we abandon God by turning to serve other things, He will turn against us and destroy us even though He has been so good to us as described in the book of Joshua. God will provide a brief moment of grace so that a few of us are allowed to survive as a remnant for God. (Joshua 24:19–24)

God is a loving God. He loves us and wants to forgive us if we just stay focused on Him. We have to understand that our sins not only affect us but what we do affects the earth. Our sins caused God to curse the earth. Many times, God had to blot out our sins just so he could even deal with our leaders. God then introduced his Son as our savior. God lets us know in the Old Testament that He needed someone else to carry our weaknesses because our religious leaders fell short. God needed to do this because we left the path that God had planned for us. God wanted to provide a way for us to be acceptable to Him. We should rejoice because God's grace puts our sins out of His sight and He clears us of guilt because we now live an honest life.

- Psalms 32:1–4 (NLT)—"Oh, what joy for those whose disobedience is forgiven, whose sin is put out of sight! Yes, what joy for those whose record the Lord has cleared of guilt, whose lives are lived in complete honesty! When I refused to confess my sin, my body wasted away, and I groaned all day long. Day and night your hand of discipline was heavy on me. My strength evaporated like water in the summer heat."

When we refuse to confess our sins, our body wastes away from all the groaning that we do all day long because the disciplining hand of God is heavy upon us. As we continue to sin, the earth has to suffer along with us. We wonder today why the earth is changing in a negative way. It's because we have twisted God's instructions and violated His covenant, therefore there is a curse that consumes the earth. We must pay the price for turning away from God, as described in the book of Isaiah.

> - Isaiah 24:4–6 (NLT)—"The earth mourns and dries up, and the crops waste away and wither. Even the greatest people on earth waste away. The earth suffers for the sins of its people, for they have twisted God's instructions, violated his laws, and broken his everlasting covenant. Therefore, a curse consumes the earth. Its people must pay the price for their sin."

God plans to destroy those who continue to sin by fire. As God deals with our rebellious ways, He even allows us to present our case if we dare to try to prove our innocence. Because of our sinful ways, God has to put decrees in place in order to address our sinful nature. God predetermined that He would send a true sacrifice. God provided one that is seen as a tender green shoot, much like a root in dry ground. The Father did not choose someone who would be attractive to us. God knew that we would turn our back on him and despise him. Yet, God charged him to carry our weaknesses, and our sorrows weighed him down. In the end, he was pierced for our rebellion, crushed for our sins, beaten so we could be whole, whipped so we could be healed, treated harshly, was led like a lamb to the slaughter, struck down for the rebellious, buried like a criminal, and he was placed in a rich man's grave. It was not man's plan to crush and cause our Lord Jesus Christ to suffer; it was the will and plan of God in order for us to have a true and unbreakable covenant with God the Father. We are all like sheep that strayed away; we have left God's path in search for our own. Yet, God laid on him the sins of the world; he was unjustly condemned and led away for our sins. Because of the obedience of our Lord Jesus Christ, we who place our trust in him will be counted righteous in God's eyes.

- Isaiah 53:2–12 (NLT)—"My servant grew up in the Lord's presence like a tender green shoot, like a root in dry ground. There was nothing beautiful or majestic about his appearance, nothing to attract us to him. He was despised and rejected—a man of sorrows, acquainted with deepest grief. We turned our backs on him and looked the other way. He was despised, and we did not care. Yet it was our weaknesses he carried; it was our sorrows that weighed him down. And we thought his troubles were a punishment from God, a punishment for his own sins! But he was pierced for our rebellion, crushed for our sins. He was beaten so we could be whole. He was whipped so we could be healed. All of us, like sheep, have strayed away. We have left God's paths to follow our own. Yet the Lord laid on him the sins of us all. He was oppressed and treated harshly, yet he never said a word. He was led like a lamb to the slaughter. And as a sheep is silent before the shearers, he did not open his mouth. Unjustly condemned, he was led away. No one cared that he died without descendants, that his life was cut short in midstream. But he was struck down for the rebellion of my people. He had done no wrong and had never deceived anyone. But he was buried like a criminal; he was put in a rich man's grave. But it was the Lord's good plan to crush him and cause him grief. Yet when his life is made an offering for sin, he will have many descendants. He will enjoy a long life, and the Lord's good plan will prosper in his hands. When he sees all that is accomplished by his anguish, he will be satisfied. And because of his experience, my righteous servant will make it possible for many to be counted righteous, for he will bear all their sins. I will give him the honors of a victorious soldier, because he exposed himself to death. He was counted among the rebels. He bore the sins of many and interceded for rebels."

God continues to request for us to return to him. He will redeem those who repent from their sins and provide His Spirit, love, and His Word to comfort us. We know that God is a jealous God and will display his anger. He just wants us to acknowledge our iniquities and transgressions and obey His Son. In the Old Testament, God rejected Israel and directed his love and passion toward Judah, but even Judah could not stay obedient to God's ways. God wants to provide us with true prosperity and peace that comes from Him. God teaches us that his ways are not our ways. He lets us know that, once we are redeemed, His Spirit will not leave us, neither will His Word. God will place His Word on the lips of those who love and seek Him.

> - Isaiah 59:20–21 (NLT)—"'The Redeemer will come to Jerusalem to buy back those in Israel who have turned from their sins,' says the Lord. 'And this is my covenant with them,' says the Lord. 'My Spirit will not leave them, and neither will these words I have given you. They will be on your lips and on the lips of your children and your children's children forever. I, the Lord, have spoken!'"

God wants us to acknowledge our guilt and admit that we have rebelled against Him. He is calling for us to return home as wayward children of God.

We need to confess that we refuse to listen to God. To help us overcome our rebellious ways, God will send us shepherds after His own heart who will guide us with knowledge and understanding. When we turn from our rebellious ways, He restores us and cleanses away our sins. When this occurs, the world will be able to see the good that God has done, and they will tremble with awe at the peace and prosperity that God has provided.

> - Jeremiah 33:6–9 (NLT)—"Nevertheless, the time will come when I will heal Jerusalem's wounds and give it prosperity and true peace. I will restore the fortunes of Judah and Israel and rebuild their towns. I will cleanse them of their sins against me and forgive all their sins of rebellion. Then this city will bring me joy, glory, and honor before all the nations of the earth! The people of the world will see all the good I do for my people, and they will tremble with awe at the peace and prosperity I provide for them."

God has a plan to bring all those who were scattered across the world back to the mountains of Israel. There is a great day of judgment and reconciliation that is coming. But, if we continue to rebel against God, great sorrow awaits us. We need to continue to cry to God with a sincere heart. We cannot look to our own strength; we have to look to the Most High for direction and counseling. As the Old Testament came to a close, God had enough of us and our religious leaders and their false prophesying, they were taking payments for their services, teaching God's ways for a price, even as they continued to claim dependency on God. Because of their sins, the anger of God was aroused, and, for 400 years, he did not communicate with man. God wants to unify us into one nation, but many of us continue to look everywhere else but to God the Most High for help. We remain crooked as a bow and useless for the work of God.

> - *Hosea 7:10–16 (NLT)—"Their arrogance testifies against them, yet they don't return to the Lord their God or even try to find him. 'The people of Israel have become like silly, witless doves, first calling to Egypt, then flying to Assyria for help. But as they fly about, I will throw my net over them and bring them down like a bird from the sky. I will punish them for all the evil they do. What sorrow awaits those who have deserted me! Let them die, for they have rebelled against me. I wanted to redeem them, but they have told lies about me. They do not cry out to me with sincere hearts. Instead, they sit on their couches and wail. They cut themselves, begging foreign gods for grain and new wine, and they turn away from me. I trained them and made them strong, yet now they plot evil against me. They look everywhere except to the Most High. They are as useless as a crooked bow. Their leaders will be killed by their enemies because of their insolence toward me.'"*

We must not continue to think that no harm will come to us because we think the Lord God is with us. We cannot continue to make decisions based on our desire for money and wealth. But there is hope if we would just turn from our rebellious ways and turn back to God. He has a plan for each one of us, a plan to set us apart and lift us up and place us on a solid foundation.

> - *Micah 3:5–7 (NLT)—"This is what the Lord says: 'You false prophets are leading my people astray! You promise peace for those who give you food, but you declare war on those who refuse to feed you. Now the night will close around you, cutting off all your visions. Darkness will cover you, putting an end to your predictions. The sun will set for you prophets, and your day will come to an end. Then you seers will be put to shame, and you*

fortune-tellers will be disgraced. And you will cover your faces because there is no answer from God."

Because God has such great love for us, he sent John the Baptist to pave the way for his Son. Jesus Christ teaches us that God has made Him the true grapevine, and God cuts off every branch that does not produce fruit, and prunes the branches that bear fruit so they can produce even more. If a branch does not bear fruit, it is severed from the vine. This lets us know that we who are in Christ Jesus, if we do not produce, we cannot remain a part of Christ's body. And we know that, outside of the Body of Christ, we can do nothing. We are thrown away if we do not work in the Body of Christ to produce good works.

> *- John 15:1–8 (NLT)—"'I am the true grapevine, and my Father is the gardener. He cuts off every branch of mine that doesn't produce fruit, and he prunes the branches that do bear fruit so they will produce even more. You have already been pruned and purified by the message I have given you. Remain in me, and I will remain in you. For a branch cannot produce fruit if it is severed from the vine, and you cannot be fruitful unless you remain in me. Yes, I am the vine; you are the branches. Those who remain in me, and I in them, will produce much fruit. For apart from me you can do nothing. Anyone who does not remain in me is thrown away like a useless branch and withers. Such branches are gathered into a pile to be burned. But if you remain in me and my words remain in you, you may ask for anything you want, and it will be granted! When you produce much fruit, you are my true disciples. This brings great glory to my Father.'"*

God provides His grace to help us get to a point where we are producing, but this does not allow us to keep on sinning under grace. Sin must lose its power over us for grace to be effective in us, thus allowing us to walk in freedom. We cannot allow sin to control the way we live or give in to its desires. Even Paul, being a very strong spiritual person, struggled with sin. But he knew that to remain in Christ, is the only way to overcome the sin within. Knowing this, should we continue to sin? Of course not!

A Life of Salvation

- Romans 6:1–8 (NLT)—"Well then, should we keep on sinning so that God can show us more and more of his wonderful grace? Of course not! Since we have died to sin, how can we continue to live in it? Or have you forgotten that when we were joined with Christ Jesus in baptism, we joined him in his death? For we died and were buried with Christ by baptism. And just as Christ was raised from the dead by the glorious power of the Father, now we also may live new lives. Since we have been united with him in his death, we will also be raised to life as he was. We know that our old sinful selves were crucified with Christ so that sin might lose its power in our lives. We are no longer slaves to sin. For when we died with Christ we were set free from the power of sin. And since we died with Christ, we know we will also live with him."

We must understand the powers that are at work in the world. There is a power that produces sin and evil, and there is also a power that produces righteous living and honor to God. These two powers are at war in our mind and body, but thank God for Jesus Christ, who defeated the power of sin and death and teaches us that we can live without being slaves to sin.

- Romans 7:18–25 (NLT)—"And I know that nothing good lives in me, that is, in my sinful nature. I want to do what is right, but I can't. I want to do what is good, but I don't. I don't want to do what is wrong, but I do it anyway. But if I do what I don't want to do, I am not really the one doing wrong; it is sin living in me that does it. I have discovered this principle of life—that when I want to do what is right, I inevitably do what is wrong. I love God's law with all my heart. But there is another power within me that is at war with my mind. This power makes me a slave to the sin that is still within me. Oh, what a miserable person I am! Who will free me from this life that is dominated by sin and death? Thank God! The answer is in Jesus Christ our Lord."

Even after we have gotten sin under control by having faith in Jesus Christ, we still must keep on trusting or we will be cut off. But God's love is always there for those who repent, for he is willing to graft those who wander away, back into his presence. We learn in Romans that God will separate from us, but if we return to Him and change our hearts after Him, He will accept us again. We must understand that, though we have accepted Christ, we must continue to believe, and we must be very careful to listen for the true Word of God, so we don't drift away.

> *- Romans 11:22–24 (NLT)—"Notice how God is both kind and severe. He is severe toward those who disobeyed, but kind to you if you continue to trust in his kindness. But if you stop trusting, you also will be cut off. And if the people of Israel turn from their unbelief, they will be grafted in again, for God has the power to graft them back into the tree. You, by nature, were a branch cut from a wild olive tree. So if God was willing to do something contrary to nature by grafting you into his cultivated tree, he will be far more eager to graft the original branches back into the tree where they belong."*

We will not escape punishment if we ignore God's plan of salvation for our life. Christ has redeemed us and called us into himself, for he paid the price with his blood. Christ has become our High Priest and entered into the Most Holy Place in heaven and secured our redemption forever. By doing this, he has offered himself up as a perfect sacrifice to God the Father for our sins. Christ provides a way for us to have a clear conscience from all the sins we have committed. We are warned to watch out that we don't lose the reward that we have worked so hard to achieve. Don't wander away; our relationship with the Father and our Lord Jesus Christ is at stake!

> *- Hebrews 2:1–3 (NLT)—"So we must listen very carefully to the truth we have heard, or we may drift away from it. For the message God delivered through angels has always stood firm, and every violation of the law and every act of disobedience was punished. So what makes us think we can escape if we ignore this great salvation that was first announced by the Lord Jesus himself and then delivered to us by those who heard him speak?"*

Our old self has been crucified with Christ and is no longer alive. We are now alive in Christ Jesus, and he lives in us. We now live in a dead body by trusting that Christ loves us and will sustain us in himself. We are comforted and strengthened through our Lord Jesus Christ in everything we do and say. Now that God's grace has been revealed to us, we are instructed to turn away from godless living and sinful pleasures. We should live in this evil world with wisdom, righteousness, and devotion, to God. We look forward to the hope of a glorious day when the glory of God the Father and our Savior Jesus Christ is revealed.

> *- Galatians 2:20–21 (NLT)—"My old self has been crucified with Christ. It is no longer I who live, but Christ lives in me. So I live in this earthly body by trusting in the Son of God, who loved me and gave himself for me. I do not treat the grace of God as meaningless. For if keeping the law could make us right with God, then there was no need for Christ to die."*

Knowing that God has granted us grace and mercy through our Lord Jesus Christ, we cannot think God's loving grace is for us to count it as meaningless, by us continuing to sin. We have received an eternal comforter, and we live with the wonderful hope of God's promises manifesting in our lives. For us to live a life under grace and full of salvation, we must stay focused on God's plan of salvation and our assignment to produce for God. We have been born again not by works but by God's grace and mercy. By grace, we are counted righteous in Christ. We must walk and live in the confidence of our faith, and we must devote ourselves to doing good.

> *- Titus 3:4–7 (NLT)—"But—'When God our Savior revealed his kindness and love, he saved us, not because of the righteous things we had done, but because of his mercy. He washed away our sins, giving us a new birth and new life through the Holy Spirit. He generously poured out the Spirit upon us through Jesus Christ our Savior. Because of his grace he declared us righteous and gave us confidence that we will inherit eternal life.'"*

Christ, our High Priest, understands what we are going through, because he himself suffered, yet He did not sin. Christ faced all the same testing we do and showed us the way to live. He knows how to provide us grace when we need it the most, as we work to overcome and please him. We must help each other and learn to live in peace with one another. We must understand that our strength comes from God's grace not by rules made up by man. We must learn to look after one another and watch out for poisonous roots of bitterness that grow up to cause trouble. We cannot become distracted or attracted by strange and new ideas; we seek the truth that comes from God's Holy Spirit.

- Hebrews 4:14–16 (NLT)—"So then, since we have a great High Priest who has entered heaven, Jesus the Son of God, let us hold firmly to what we believe. This High Priest of ours understands our weaknesses, for he faced all of the same testings we do, yet he did not sin. So let us come boldly to the throne of our gracious God. There we will receive his mercy, and we will find grace to help us when we need it most."

In the book of James, we are taught that friendship with the world makes us enemies of God. We cannot spend our time, money, and energy seeking the things that are in this world. It's important that we are not divided between the cares of this world and God. He wants us to learn how to become and stay humble. We are taught to humble ourselves before God the Father and Jesus Christ, and, when we resist the devil, he has to flee from us. We need to come closer to God, and He will draw closer to us. We know that God looks at our hearts and not our words and actions to determine if we love Him. The more we draw closer to God, the more grace, peace, and joy he grants us. By us doing the things that please God, He will lift us up out from the reaches of a sinful world and out of the reach of the devil. We must constantly remember that God knew us before we were created and He chose us. Because we have accepted His calling and not rebelled, we can receive His Holy Spirit.

- James 4:4–6 (NLT)—"You adulterers! Don't you realize that friendship with the world makes you an enemy of God? I say it again: If you want to be a friend of the world, you make yourself an enemy of God. What do you think the Scriptures mean when they say that the spirit God has placed within us is filled with envy? But he gives us even more grace to stand against such evil desires."

We are continually warned to stay alert. Satan is looking to deceive those who believe in God the Father and our Lord Jesus Christ. We are all suffering to refuse the tricks and schemes of the devil. God doesn't want us to suffer long, just long enough for us to acknowledge Him even in our troubles and trials. He will restore, support, and strengthen us as we overcome this world. He will place us on a firm foundation.

- 1 Peter 5:8–11 (NLT)—"Stay alert! Watch out for your great enemy, the devil. He prowls around like a roaring lion, looking for someone to devour. Stand firm against him, and be strong in your faith. Remember that your Christian brothers and sisters all over the world are going through the same kind of suffering you are. In his kindness God called you to share in his eternal glory by means of Christ Jesus. So after you have suffered a little while, he will restore, support, and strengthen you, and he will place you on a firm foundation. All power to him forever! Amen."

Again, we are warned about not being carried away by teaching errors and wicked people; we can lose our footing and fall. We need to be on guard. We must grow and produce under the grace that we have been granted and in the knowledge of our savior, Jesus Christ. There are people who have joined churches for the purpose of deceiving God's people.

- 2 Peter 3:17–18 (NLT)—"I am warning you ahead of time, dear friends. Be on guard so that you will not be carried away by the errors of these wicked people and lose your own secure footing. Rather, you must grow in the grace and knowledge of our Lord and Savior Jesus Christ."

They teach that, because we have been granted grace through our Lord Jesus, we can continue to live immoral and sinful lifestyles. There are those who claim authority based on their dreams, thinking God is speaking to them, but in reality, Satan is the one whispering in their ears. When we are living a repented lifestyle, we are empowered by the Holy Spirit to do great things in Christ, to God's glory. If we are producing godly fruit, we are living a life of salvation. We know this is true because we work every day to abide in Christ. We also know this because there is no bitterness, rage, anger, harsh words, slander, evil behavior, sexual immorality, impurity, or greed in us. We know because others see a tenderhearted, forgiving, giving, and loving person. We are the ones who allow the Holy Spirit to control our behavior and tongue. A life of salvation is based on us walking in the light, walking protected, wearing the full armor of God. Others will know we are walking in a life of salvation because they will see we no longer participate in the foolish, wild, and destructive things we use to do. A life of salvation is about walking in the spirit, praying in the spirit, being at peace, seeking God's will, confessing, and overcoming our sins as God the Father and our Lord Jesus Christ reveals that which needs to be cleansed within us. By seeking and staying on God's plan of salvation, we can avoid losing our place in Christ and having to work our way back to being grafted back on to the vine of life.

> *- Jude 1:4–10 (NLT)*—*"I say this because some ungodly people have wormed their way into your churches, saying that God's marvelous grace allows us to live immoral lives. The condemnation of such people was recorded long ago, for they have denied our only Master and Lord, Jesus Christ. So I want to remind you, though you already know these things, that Jesus first rescued the nation of Israel from Egypt, but later he destroyed those who did not remain faithful. And I remind you of the angels who did not stay within the limits of authority God gave them but left the place where they belonged. God has kept them securely chained in prisons of darkness, waiting for the great day of judgment. And don't forget Sodom and Gomorrah and their neighboring towns, which were filled with immorality and every kind of sexual perversion. Those cities were destroyed by fire and serve as a warning of the eternal fire of God's judgment. In the same way, these people—who claim authority from their dreams—live immoral lives, defy authority, and scoff at supernatural beings. But even Michael, one of the mightiest of the angels, did not dare accuse the devil of blasphemy, but simply said, "The Lord rebuke you!" (This took place when Michael was arguing with the devil about Moses' body.) But these people scoff at things they do not understand. Like unthinking animals, they do whatever their instincts tell them, and so they bring about their own destruction."*

A Life of Salvation

How Do We Live a Life of Salvation?

It's important for us to understand the type of protection our Lord Jesus Christ and God the Father provides if we work to stay in his mercy and grace. We know that we are living under God's salvation because we live through our Lord Jesus Christ. We are not just going around saying that we are "saved", because we know that this means nothing to God.

> - Matthew 3:7–9 (NLT)—"But when he saw many Pharisees and Sadducees coming to watch him baptize, he denounced them. 'You brood of snakes!' he exclaimed. 'Who warned you to flee God's coming wrath? Prove by the way you live that you have repented of your sins and turned to God. Don't just say to each other, "We're safe, for we are descendants of Abraham." That means nothing, for I tell you, God can create children of Abraham from these very stones.'"

We prove that we love God the Father and our Lord Jesus Christ by the way we live. We are then granted the ability to handle snakes, overcome poisonous drinks, heal the sick, speak in new languages, cast out demons, and receive eternal life. We will not perish, nor can anyone take us away from Christ. Again, we are reminded that we must work to keep Christ's commandments. If we abide in Him, we will remain in His great joy and peace.

> - Mark 16:14–18 (NLT)—"Still later he appeared to the eleven disciples as they were eating together. He rebuked them for their stubborn unbelief because they refused to believe those who had seen him after he had been raised from the dead. And then he told them, 'Go into all the world and preach the Good News to everyone. Anyone who believes and is baptized will be saved. But anyone who refuses to believe will be condemned. These miraculous signs will accompany those who believe: They will cast out demons in my name, and they will speak in new languages. They will be able to handle snakes with safety, and if they drink anything poisonous, it won't hurt them. They will be able to place their hands on the sick, and they will be healed.'"

A Life of Salvation

Through a life of continuously seeking God, growing in the body of Christ, learning and listening to the Holy Spirit, and encouraging and connecting others to Christ, we will experience the true plan of God's salvation in our life. We will receive that experience when Jesus Christ comes to give us our reward, but right now, in the middle of a dying world, in the midst of those who only experience God from a religious experience, in the midst of those who don't believe that God the Father and our Lord Jesus Christ exist, we, who totally surrender our lives to Jesus Christ, will experience becoming a new creation. We will experience the oneness of God the Father and our Lord Jesus Christ because we are now one with Jesus Christ and God the Father. We have been transformed, based on the Spirit of God, into the image of Christ.

> - John 10:27–30 (NLT)—"My sheep listen to my voice; I know them, and they follow me. I give them eternal life, and they will never perish. No one can snatch them away from me, for my Father has given them to me, and he is more powerful than anyone else. No one can snatch them from the Father's hand. The Father and I are one."

Knowing that the Holy Spirit resides in us, we have to be careful not to grieve the Holy Spirit with our transgressions. We must get rid of all bitterness, rage, anger, harsh words, and slander, to ensure that we don't cause God's spirit to leave us. We must imitate Christ by not having any sexual immorality, impurity, greed, foolish talk, or coarse joking, in us. We cannot be fooled by those who make excuses for their sin. We understand that such sins have no place among the people of God. We don't even participate in what these evil people do; we take no part in the worthless and darkness that they like to enjoy and live in. We are children of light, and we must walk in the light. We must understand that it is shameful for us to even talk about the things ungodly people do in secret. Those who have evil intentions will be exposed when Christ's light is shined on them, for it will make everything visible. We must put on the full armor of God, the belt of truth, the breastplate of righteousness, the shoes of peace, the shield of faith, the helmet of salvation, and the sword of the spirit. We need to always be in prayer seeking the will of our Lord Jesus Christ and God the Father with all supplications in the Spirit.

- Ephesians 4:25–32 (NLT)—"So stop telling lies. Let us tell our neighbors the truth, for we are all parts of the same body. And 'don't sin by letting anger control you.' Don't let the sun go down while you are still angry, for anger gives a foothold to the devil. If you are a thief, quit stealing. Instead, use your hands for good hard work, and then give generously to others in need. Don't use foul or abusive language. Let everything you say be good and helpful, so that your words will be an encouragement to those who hear them. And do not bring sorrow to God's Holy Spirit by the way you live. Remember, he has identified you as his own, guaranteeing that you will be saved on the day of redemption. Get rid of all bitterness, rage, anger, harsh words, and slander, as well as all types of evil behavior. Instead, be kind to each other, tenderhearted, forgiving one another, just as God through Christ has forgiven you."

We must remain watchful all the way until the end because we know temptation will continue to press upon our spirits to test and deceive us. The Word of God is not about any one person having all the knowledge, so we must avoid quarrels and arguments over the Word of God. People doing these types of things turn away from God's truth, and their sins will condemn them. We are not like those who turn away from God to their own destruction. We are the faithful ones, whose lives will be saved.

- Ephesians 6:10–12 (NLT)—"A final word: Be strong in the Lord and in his mighty power. Put on all of God's armor so that you will be able to stand firm against all strategies of the devil. For we are not fighting against flesh-and-blood enemies, but against evil rulers and authorities of the unseen world, against mighty powers in this dark world, and against evil spirits in the heavenly places."

- Titus 3:9–11 (NLT)—"Do not get involved in foolish discussions about spiritual pedigrees or in quarrels and fights about obedience to Jewish laws. These things are useless and a waste of time. If people are causing divisions among you, give a first and second warning. After that, have nothing more to do with them. For people

like that have turned away from the truth, and their own sins condemn them."

We must all be quick to listen, slow to speak, and slow to get angry. Anger does not produce the righteousness God desires. So we have to get rid of all the filth and evil in our lives and humbly accept the Word of God that is planted in our hearts, for it has the power to save our souls. We can't just listen to God's Word, but we must do what it says. Otherwise, we are only fooling ourselves. We have to understand that faith should produce good works out of us. If we are blessed and see our brothers and sisters struggling, and all we do is pray that they are blessed when we could have blessed them, then we are fooling ourselves into thinking we are being Godly toward them. We are charged to feed and clothe the poor. Just having faith is not enough; we must allow our faith to produce and be willing to share with others. We must obey the whole Word of God and not pick and choose what we will or will not believe in, when it comes to applying God's Word to our everyday lives. The whole Word of God is to strengthen our relationship and walk with Him and our Savior Jesus Christ.

- James 1:19–22 (NLT)—"Understand this, my dear brothers and sisters: You must all be quick to listen, slow to speak, and slow to get angry. Human anger does not produce the righteousness God desires. So get rid of all the filth and evil in your lives, and humbly accept the word God has planted in your hearts, for it has the power to save your souls. But don't just listen to God's word. You must do what it says. Otherwise, you are only fooling yourselves."

What does it mean to suffer for Christ? It begins with us having the same attitude as Christ, and it ends when we have poured our lives, to complete our assignment on earth. We cannot spend the rest of our lives chasing our own desires; we must be eager to do God's will every day. We cannot be intimidated in any way by our enemies. We, as members of the Body of Christ, are in this struggle together.

- Philippians 1:28–30 (NLT)—"Don't be intimidated in any way by your enemies. This will be a sign to them that they are going to be destroyed, but that you are going to be saved, even by God

himself. For you have been given not only the privilege of trusting in Christ but also the privilege of suffering for him. We are in this struggle together. You have seen my struggle in the past, and you know that I am still in the midst of it."

Those around us will think it strange that we no longer engage in the wild and destructive things we use to do. We all will face God, who will judge both the living and the dead. We should be happy when we are insulted for living a life of salvation as Christians. We suffer because we work to do good, walking in peace, not committing sin as the world. We no longer indulge in murder, stealing, making trouble, or prying into other people's affairs. What trouble awaits those who never obeyed God's Good News! Since everything around us will be destroyed, we are looking forward to a new heaven and a new earth. While we are waiting for these things to happen, make every effort to be found living peaceful lives that are pure and blameless in Christ's sight. To him who overcomes, Christ will grant a seat on His throne; as Christ also overcame and sat down with the Father on His throne. A life of salvation is a privilege to suffer with Christ. If we stay faithful, in the end, we will enter into the Kingdom of God, led by our Savior Jesus Christ. What a wonderful day that will be for those who walk by faith.

> *- 1 Peter 4:4–6 (NLT)—"Of course, your former friends are surprised when you no longer plunge into the flood of wild and destructive things they do. So they slander you. But remember that they will have to face God, who will judge everyone, both the living and the dead. That is why the Good News was preached to those who are now dead—so although they were destined to die like all people, they now live forever with God in the Spirit.*

Becoming saved is just the beginning. We have a lifetime to learn God's ways and His will for our lives. Once we are saved from our past sins, we need to continue to abide in Christ, to stay covered in God's grace and mercy. He will reveal the things we need to work on and those things we are called to do; all to the glory of God the Father and our Lord Jesus Christ. A life of salvation is what we are seeking; we are not just trying to slide

A Life of Salvation

into the Kingdom of God, thinking grace will cover our sinful ways. We are children of God, called to be holy and humble, always seeking his face in all we do, think, and produce. To the glory of God the Father and our Lord Jesus Christ. Amen.

Prayer of Salvation

I come to you Father God,
And to you Lord Christ Jesus on my knees.
I come to confess my sins.
I come asking for forgiveness
For having the spirit of Hate.
I come asking for forgiveness
For having a Jealous spirit.
I come asking for forgiveness
For having a Selfish Spirit.
I come asking for forgiveness
For having a Lying Spirit.
I come asking for forgiveness
For having a Cursing Spirit.
I come asking for forgiveness
For causing others so much Pain and Suffering.
I come asking for forgiveness
Please accept me as I am, and make me into
What you want and have planned for me to be
Thank you for your grace and mercy
Thank you for saving a person like me

A Life of Salvation

The purpose of this chart is to provide a visual understanding of the content in this chapter. The reader can use this chart to help develop a holistic view of living a life of salvation. It describes the process of working on our salvation and the process involved in achieving the goal of entering into the Kingdom of God. It shares the effects of committing transgressions against God, and the results of us turning away from God the Father and our Lord Jesus Christ. It gives a picture of living in the body of Christ and how we must overcome sin by being changed and transformed into the image of Jesus Christ. It also helps the reader see the need for God to continue to grant us grace and mercy as we work on our salvation in Jesus Christ. The chart presents a picture of the coming of judgment day and the entering of those who are at rest in God and those who have died in their sin into the judgment of Christ. The last part of the chart shares how those who have made it through, enter into the Kingdom of God, compared to those who fail to make it into God's Kingdom and their designation of the lake of fire. We hope the reader would use this chart to help assess where they are in their walk with God and be able to move forward to achieve the prize of entering into the Kingdom of God.

A Life of Salvation

A LIFE OF SALVATION

The Body Of Christ Colossians 1:22

Grace and Mercy Hebrews 4:16

All the start we continue to transgress against the Father, Jesus Christ, and the Holy Spirit.

As Transformation & Change continues in us, we stop sinning and become like Christ.

God's Plans — Your Plans

Transformation & Change Romans 12:2 — Overcoming 1 John 5:3 — Transgression

Sin — Doubt — Unbelief — Sin

Your Desires Galatians 5:19

God's Kingdom

Reaching and Bringing Others to Christ Romans 15:2

Transformation & Change James 4:16 — Overcoming — Transgression

Your Desires

God's Kingdom

Transformation & Change — Overcoming — Transgression Proverbs 29:6

Your Desires

God's Kingdom

Turning from God & Christ Revelation 3:3

Turning from God & Christ

Reject the Word of God

Finishing the Race Philippians 3:14

- Belief in God the Father
- Acceptance of Jesus Christ
- Confession
- Baptism
- Receiving the Holy Spirit
- Repent

"Saved" Accepted by God and Jesus Christ Romans 10:8

The Word of God Luke 11:28
Faith 1 Peter 1:9
Holy Spirit Luke 11:13
Love of God Romans 8:39

Romans 10:17

Sin, Doubt, or Unbelief = Lack of Faith

The Beginning to Keeping the Word of God

We are able to help others understand the Transformation process

Your Plans
Unbelief Hebrews 3:19 — Sin — Sin
Doubt Mark 11:23
Your Desires — Sin

You may or may not have some understanding of God and Christ

Their Plans
Sin — Sin — Sin
Their Desires — Sin

They may or may not have some understanding of God and Christ

- No Faith
- No Belief
- Full of Doubt
- No Truth
- No Love

Judgment Jude 1:15

The Believer — Enter Into

The Non-Believer — Thrown Into

God's Rest
Paradise Hebrews 4:10

Rejecting the Body of Christ
Hebrews 6:6

The Reward
Colossians 3:25

The Kingdom of God
Luke 18:25

Lake of Fire
Revelation 20:15

Conclusion

After looking back on my life and the spiritual transformation that has taken place, it is a blessing that God would take the time to reach into the fire and snatch a sinner such as myself out of the burning flames. There are no words to compare the power of His saving grace and mercy. While many of us experience different situations and circumstances as we draw closer to God the Father and our Lord Jesus Christ, things that God put in place remain the same. God the Father gave us a true God in Jesus Christ and has equipped us with His loving Holy Spirit to lead us into His Kingdom. It's just a matter of how much we are willing to believe and place our faith in God so we can fully experience A Life of Salvation. Are we willing to allow the Holy Spirit to teach us the truth about God without any religious overtones that could block the truth from our ears? There is nothing wrong with becoming connected to God through a religious organization, but the religious organization cannot become your God. We are to seek a right relationship with God the Father through our Lord Jesus Christ. There is no other way to the Father, except through Jesus Christ His Son. We have to keep alert and be aware of what we hear and listen to in these last days because the prophecy of the Bible will come true, because it's a promise from God. Seek Him in every way; He will answer and come in and be with you. We need to count the cost so we can understand what it takes and be willing to pay the full price for entry into the Kingdom of God. Just as he was made to suffer, we too must suffer. Those who are faithful will be counted as righteous before God. In the end, we all can possess the love of God in us. We must not only love God, we must be in love with God, our Lord Jesus Christ, and the Word of God. Go into the world and demonstrate the Love of God that is in you every day. Amen.

I have received some powerful teaching from God, and I am instructed to share some of these teachings in three books to help God's people continue to serve our Lord Jesus Christ in truth and in godly love. We must develop a personal responsibility to Christ Jesus and allow God's Holy Spirit to prepare us for the coming of Our Lord and God's Kingdom.

A Life of Salvation—This is the first of three books that helps readers with their journey to experience a personal relationship with God. I pray that you allow the Holy Spirit to enter into your circumstances and situations so you can be free to experience the fullness of God's plan in your life. A Life of Salvation, which provides love, peace, and joy.

Forth Coming:

God's Loving Ways—This is the second of three books that shares with readers the loving ways of God, for those who are personally seeking Him. The purpose of this book to guide readers through God's ways in dealing with such subjects as God's love, our thinking, why we were created, and the power of prayer.

Christ's Church—This is the last of three books, which shares with readers the structure of the church as defined by Word of God, Christ's purpose for the , and the apostles' role in setting clear doctrine that positions those in the church to worship and praise Christ in truth and love. We can never be confused regarding who is the head of the church.

About the Author

Minister Cecil Barry has been called by God to share powerful teachings that have changed and transformed his life, and the lives of others. At the age of 26, he committed himself to Christ Jesus, has been dedicated the past 10 years, developing a personal relationship with God the Father and our Lord Jesus Christ, learning to hear and follow the voice of God. He has now been instructed to "Go" and share what has been taught to him with others. He has been called to preach the Word of God, connect individuals to Christ, and help grow fellow believers into a mature Christian walk with Jesus Christ. The mission given to him is to teach the Word of God to both beginners in Christ and to those who are ready for spiritual transformation. His passion is to spread the love and the compassion of God, to believers and nonbelievers. Minister Barry was born in Dallas, Texas, and resides in Frisco, Texas. Currently, he is a member of Kingdom Life Fellowship located in McKinney, Texas, where he leads the men's ministry, preaches, and supports Sunday morning bible study. And he loves to teach about God's loving ways. He works with the prison ministry of North Dallas Community Fellowship church, which visits Oklahoma area prisons to preach and teach the Word of God to inmates. He also leads a workplace Bible study group at his current place of employment. Minister Barry is working on his Doctor of Ministry degree at Colorado Theology Seminary. God has blessed him with a loving wife, Donna, and his beautiful daughter, Ti'Ara. God has directed Minister Barry to launch a church in Little Elm, Texas, to help spread the teaching of the Word of God.